Toiles for All Seasons
French & English Printed Textiles
STARR SIEGELE

BUNKER HILL PUBLISHING
BOSTON

in association with
ALLENTOWN ART MUSEUM

To my mother and hers,
Claire Louise Siegele and Louise Starr

www.bunkerhillpublishing.com

First published in 2004 by Bunker Hill Publishing Inc.
26 Adams Street, Charlestown, MA 02129 USA

10 9 8 7 6 5 4 3 2 1

Library of Congress Control Number: 2004103204

ISBN 1 59373 030 6

Designed by Louise Millar

Printed in China

Endpapers *Jean-Baptiste Huët for Oberkampf Manuf.*, Les Délices des quatre saisons
(The Delights of the Four Seasons), c. 1785, full repeat, Jouy-en-Josas, France.

Title page *Detail of* The Four Seasons, *after 1793, England.*

Unless otherwise noted, all fabrics illustrated here are copperplate-printed cotton, plain weave.

Foreword

This publication coincides with two important anniversaries at the Allentown Art Museum: the fortieth anniversary of the founding of our volunteer organization, the Society of the Arts (SOTA), and the thirtieth anniversary of the Kate Fowler Merle-Smith gift of textiles. Two years after SOTA's founding, it established a fund to purchase fine art prints to complement the Museum's core Old Master collection of Samuel H. Kress paintings, along with its other collections of painting, sculpture, and decorative arts. Over the last four decades, the SOTA Print Fund has made possible an admirable range of outstanding acquisitions, including rarities, such as the miniature portrait designs that are published in this book (figs. 51-52).

In 1974, Kate Fowler Merle-Smith donated 2,500 textiles collected during her world travels in the early part of the twentieth century. Because the Merle-Smith collection did not include printed toiles, several textiles in her gift were traded for early furnishing prints with New York textile dealer Cora Ginsburg. Among these traded items is the fine *Les Eléments*, designed by Marie-Bonaventure Lebert for Hartmann's firm in Munster (fig. 54). Then, in 2002, the Museum purchased at auction a group of early French printed toiles from the estate of Elinor Merrell. This influential dealer-collector had a passionate knowledge of the subject, and she had advised and helped build the world-class collections of printed textiles at some of America's leading museums, including The Metropolitan Museum of Art, Museum of Fine Arts, Boston, and the Art Institute of Chicago. While, ultimately, the majority of works in Merrell's collection were bequeathed to the Cooper-Hewitt National Design Museum, which is part of the Smithsonian Institution, several fine duplicate works, including Allentown's *Diane et Endymion*, were sold to benefit the Smithsonian. Through this recent acquisition, the Allentown Art Museum's collection now numbers some seventy printed toiles.

Allentown's print collection has been very ably built by Starr Siegele, the Museum's adjunct curator of prints since 1984. Fortuitously, Siegele's research interests have led to groundbreaking discoveries concerning the relationship between printed works on paper and cloth. She has pursued these scholarly interests as Research Curator for Printed Textiles at the Art Institute of Chicago (1995-2000), Veronika Gervers Fellow, Royal Ontario Museum (2000), and as Leo and Julia Forchheimer Fellow (2000-2001) and Samuel H. Kress Foundation Research Scholar (2002-03), both at The Metropolitan Museum of Art's Antonio Ratti Textile Center in New York.

By helping to fund this publication, The Kress Foundation has continued to support both Siegele's work and the Allentown Art Museum. As 2004 marks the Foundation's seventy-fifth year, we are pleased to celebrate their anniversary, and the the significant milestones at our own institution, with the publication of *Toiles for All Seasons*. The Museum is also grateful to Peggy and Bill Hecht for their generous support of this publication.

This book places Allentown's collection of printed toiles in an international context. Siegele's narrative is ingeniously arranged in a lively, poetic sequence to echo the progression of an important text from the eighteenth century: James Thomson's *The Seasons*, 1730. The book will reward the beginning reader seeking knowledge about the origins of printed textiles; collectors, curators, and scholars of the period's social history, literature, and theatre will gain from Siegele's years of international travel and research into the complex relationships among artists and textile firms in the eighteenth and early nineteenth centuries.

DAVID R. BRIGHAM
THE PRISCILLA PAYNE HURD EXECUTIVE DIRECTOR
ALLENTOWN ART MUSEUM

Manuf. unknown, The Four Seasons, *after 1793, full repeat, England. This design is adapted from* Spring *and* Summer, *painted by Charles Catton II (1756-1819), and* Autumn *and* Winter *painted by Richard Corbould (1757-1831) from their engraved illustrations by Francis Chesham (1749-1806) for James Thomson,* The Seasons *(Perth, Scotland: R. Morison and Son, 1793).*

4

Introduction

Toile designs delight tastemakers today just as they did in the late eighteenth and early nineteenth centuries. The scenes printed on these early cottons or linen-cotton blends often evoke a charmed existence spent in harmony with the seasons, where gods and goddesses, milkmaids and their swains, play out Rococo and Neoclassical fantasies. Manufactured today—as well as yesterday—for clothing, upholstery, draperies, and wall coverings, *toiles-de-Jouy*, chintz, and calico have experienced the cycle of fashion, and they now enjoy a second springtime. So too does their early history, from the 1750s through about 1830, parallel nature's cycle from spring to winter. Those "seasons" in the evolution of the printed cotton industry—with their artists and entrepreneurs, aesthetic changes and technical breakthroughs—are our subject here.

The subjects figuring in scenic toiles are also of interest. Only recently has it become clear to what extent they reflect all aspects of life in the late eighteenth and early nineteenth centuries. Once thought to be merely decorative, these charming prints, produced with carved wood blocks or copperplate engravings, depicted everything from historic and current events to popular and even censored theatre and literature. Through their images, we can trace changing fashions in dress, trends in architecture and gardening, and the latest theories of rearing and educating children. The famous appear in glory or defeat, and it is even possible to glean which types of pictures the art market was encouraging collectors to buy. Still more astonishing is the ingenious and seemingly natural combination of many of these subjects within the same design. The early pictures printed on toiles provide fascinating puzzles that challenge us to interpret a once-familiar visual language from our distance of two and a half centuries.

The keys to understanding are the engraved models that the textile designers almost always used as their guides and inspirations. Artists themselves avidly collected prints from all periods, and printed textile manufacturers kept lending libraries of them to circulate among their designers. In fact, relationships between the textile printing and printmaking businesses were symbiotic. So, the first step in interpretation is finding a connection between a specific image printed on fabric and its counterpart on paper. If the context in which the printed model was produced is clear, we can often deduce the textile designer's motive in borrowing a given image at a specific time.

Before the invention of photography in the mid-1830s, prints—meaning woodcuts, etchings, engravings, and mezzotints—were the only means of reproducing visual information for wide circulation. People assembled encyclopedic collections of prints to inform themselves about everything from the tiniest insect to the loftiest gods, from the configuration of flowers to the workings of human anatomy, from the images of rulers to maps of the world. Everything that could be seen or imagined was represented in prints.

The eighteenth century has been called an Age of Enlightenment for the overall brilliance of its

1. Copper roller engraved with the pattern, Diane Chasseresse *(Diana, the huntress), which is displayed on the bed in the background and in fig. 41. The roller is an exact replica of a nineteenth-century example.*

thought, and especially for its advances in science, technology, exploration, and archaeology. So it is not unusual to imagine enlightened citizens wanting to surround themselves with the most interesting and pleasing images of the day. These might take the form of engraved book illustrations, prints made for collectors to display in their homes or paste into albums, and, by the middle of the eighteenth century, printed textiles for interior decoration. By the 1750s, textile manufacturers had learned how to print colorfast designs on washable cotton and linen using carved woodblock stamps, and they began producing the first scenic furnishing fabrics printed with engraved copper plates. Perhaps the idea of counting sheep to induce sleep comes from that era, when, for the first time, walls, curtains, upholstered chairs, and especially elaborate canopy beds were covered and draped with scenes of shepherds and their flocks in idyllic landscapes strewn with ancient ruins.

It is precisely because there were so many ideas and themes represented in printed toiles that this book is organized in a synthesizing fashion. Around the same time that colorfast printing on cotton began as a major industry in Great Britain and Europe, everyone was avidly reading an unusual, book-length poem about nature. It was novel in the way it bridged naturalistic description and allegory, and the intensely vivid pictures it evoked captivated everyone who read it. The poet presented the cycle of the four seasons as an overarching symbol that encompassed other natural rhythmic patterns, such as the times of day and the stages of human growth. Also part of the equation were the elements essential to life—earth, air, fire, and water—and the stars and planets of the Zodiac, which were thought to govern and unify heaven and earth. All four of James Thomson's poems were published together

for the first time in 1730 as *The Seasons*. Over the next century the book was translated into numerous foreign languages, interpreted in an oratorio by Joseph Hayden, and given at least nineteen different sets of engraved illustrations for its many editions. The poem had an acknowledged effect on a wide range of cultural developments in literature, painting, and music: textile design was hardly exempt. The frontispiece and headpieces for the chapters of this book clearly reveal the debt of one English toile designer to illustrations in an edition of *The Seasons* published in Perth in 1793.[1] Although the other printed textiles reproduced here may not borrow as directly from the poem's illustrations, it becomes clear that many of their images were inspired by Thomson's poem.

From the copperplate-printed cottons produced for the nobility in the mid-eighteenth century to the affordable, engraved roller-printed fabrics mass-produced after about 1800 **(fig 1)**, these home furnishings were the fashionable material of everyday domestic life, and their designs had a subtle, gently insistent way of reflecting and shaping taste. While we trace how the business of printing colorfast dress goods and soft home furnishings developed into a major industry in Britain, and especially in France, we will examine a few of the designs with regard to their underlying models. Some of the more famous personalities associated with their production will be presented, and homage will be paid to the skill with which the best designers not only mined and adapted the art of their own time but also appropriated work made in the seventeenth century, the Italian Renaissance, and ancient Rome. In placing some of these printed toiles in context, a clearer picture will emerge of the historic, social, and cultural significance they may have held for their fortunate original owners.

2. *Detail of Charles Emmanuel Perregaux for Pourtales et Cie,* La Pêche et le Commerce Maritime *(Fishing and Maritime Trade), c. 1787. Underscoring the international character of the early printed textile industry, this textile resulted from a commission given by a Swiss manufacturer from Neuchâtel to a Genevan engraver living in Bourgoin, France. The pattern reverses one produced by Oberkampf's French factory at Jouy-en-Josas earlier in the 1780s (see note 2).*

Prologue

The story of modern printed fabrics begins in Europe in medieval times, before paper was widely used in the Western world, nearly a half-century before the printing press was invented. Our knowledge about the early history of printed cloth is scant, because so few examples survive.[2] Among the most complete is a church lectern cloth woven of linen in the beginning of the 1400s at Salzburg **(fig. 4)**. Stamped from carved wood blocks, inked in brown, and further enhanced with painted colors, the design reveals the resourcefulness of its artist, who aligned repeating decorative elements to form a continuous, interlocking pattern around the main image, the New Testament story of Jesus miraculously turning water into wine for the wedding feast in Cana. Since so few people living at the beginning of the fifteenth century knew how to read, this cloth, suspended from a lectern in full view of the congregation, was intended to provide a visual meditation for illiterate worshippers. It was a poor man's substitute for richer tapestries and embroideries.

In 1592, an English ship captured a Portuguese trade vessel bearing wondrous cargo from India. News of this exotic treasure must have traveled exceedingly fast for those days, and it extolled the exotic, gaily painted and printed cotton fabrics that miraculously kept their colors through washing **(fig. 5)**. The find inspired imitations, and within a year, an ambitious Italian artist printed an extraordinary series of sumptuous woodcuts on purple silk, high-

3. Wood block for printing fabric, second half of the eighteenth century, France. The flowering branches are carved in relief against a dotted background pattern formed by tiny metal pins (picotage). To create linear details, thin metal strips could be substituted for these pins, and for a solid ground, a layer of felt could be glued onto the block, which generally measured less than a foot in either direction. A separate block was cut for each color in the design.

9

4. The Marriage at Cana, *c. 1400-1420, Tyrol, Upper Austria around Salzburg, linen, wood-block-printed and hand-colored. This lectern cloth reminds us that printing on fabric helped lead to printing on paper, which early on was actually rags macerated into pulp and pressed into sheets.*

5. *Palampore, c. 1775, Coromandel Coast, India, linen twill weave, wood-block-printed and hand-painted. Although printed later, this Indian bedspread illustrates the same printing process (and has a similar floral design) as that used on the earliest import, which survives only in descriptions.*

11

6. *Detail of Magdalena Van de Passe,* Salmacis and a Hermaphrodite, *1623, Utrecht, etching and engraving on paper.*

lighted them by hand in gold, and presented them to the duke of Mantua.[3] Clearly, Indian calicoes (so called because they were made around Calcutta) captured imaginations throughout Europe. Their desirability quickly led to the formation of several East India trading companies as the demand for chintz (from an Indian word meaning "stained" or "speckled") grew unabated for the next century and a half, despite attempts by European textile manufacturers to provide less costly reproductions, and despite prohibitions on the import and production of cotton cloth instigated by the silk and wool industries' strong political lobbies.[4]

The next development in printed fabrics occurred in both their content and form. Some recently discovered patent documents from the 1630s reveal that one particularly enterprising Dutch engraver started her own business printing political motifs and other timely images on cloth sleeping caps[5]—a forebear of the ubiquitous printed T-shirts of today's popular market. Magdalena Van de Passe (1600-1638) engraved the designs on copper and used the same oil-based pigments and intaglio press her family employed in their Utrecht printing firm **(fig. 6).** But those inks tended to leave an offensive odor that lingered in fabric, and the caps could not be washed effectively. No caps survive, but they set the precedent for printing topical themes on fabrics for clothing. Around the time of Magdalena's death, Armenians or Turks from the Near East supposedly revealed some of the mysteries of colorfast dyeing techniques to the West. It is known that by 1648 a maker of playing cards in Marseilles, Benoît Gantheaume, teamed up with the engraver Jacques Baville to establish a business printing bedspreads using colorfast dyeing techniques. Following them over the next thirty-some years, firms in England, Holland, Germany, and Switzerland began adapting India's tedious methods of woodblock printing using starch- or gum-thickened metallic mordant salts to fix the dyes to fabric. Nevertheless, colorfast technology for dyeing plate-engraved pictures on cloth would elude the abilities of Western textile manufacturers until the 1750s.

7. Spring, *from James Thomson,* The Seasons *(Perth ed., 1793), engraving by Francis Chesham after a painting by Charles Catton II.*

ONE
Spring

Come, gentle Spring, Ethereal Mildness,
come . . . .
Delightful task! To rear the Tender thought,
To teach the young idea to shoot. . . .

James Thomson, *"Spring,"* The Seasons

8. Detail of Frontispiece: Spring, *from* The Four Seasons *textile, after 1793.*

9. Jean-Baptiste Huët, probably for Oberkampf Manuf., Apollo in his Chariot Transforms Night into Day, c. 1787, pen and brown ink, brush and gray wash with pale orange watercolor, black chalk on cream laid paper. Apollo's Chariot of the Dawn, surrounded by dancers representing the progression of hours and seasons, signals the beginning of day and of springtime, reflecting specific imagery in James Thomson's book-length poem, The Seasons.

> But Yonder comes the powerful King of Day,
> Rejoicing in the East...
> Parent of the Seasons !..
> While, round thy beaming Car,
> High-seen, the Seasons lead, in sprightly Dance
> Harmonious knit, the rosy-finger'd Hours.
>
> *James Thomson, "Summer"* The Seasons

For a dawning industry that would rapidly exert undreamed of economic influence, there was a key year—one that, in retrospect, is aptly symbolized by a bold Apollo driving his chariot of the Dawn **(fig. 9)**.[6] It was 1752. During the early eighteenth century, the well-to-do of Europe flaunted clothing that was woodblock printed in floral, striped, and geometric patterns **(figs. 10-11)**. They were defying English and French laws against the import, production, and purchase of printed cottons. But their taste encouraged a pivotal invention that would propel cotton printing into a powerful orbit. In 1752, Francis Nixon (d. 1765), a printer working in Drumcondra, near Dublin, devised a method for mordant dyeing using engraved copperplates, and within four years he had passed the process to a London merchant.[8]

Nixon's advance made it possible to cover three times more fabric—up to a square meter—with a single run through the printing press. And the sophisticated pictures afforded by finely detailed engraving techniques completely transformed the aesthetic scope of printed textile design. As a result, all the

10. *Lady's open robe made in England of fabric from the Coromandel Coast, India, 1740-1750, cotton with hand-painted and resist-dyed polychrome floral pattern (designed for the European market).*

11. *Infant's dress, Coromandel Coast, India, eighteenth century, cotton, wood-block-printed, mordant-painted, and immersion-dyed.*

17

12. *Robert Jones, Old Ford Manuf.,* Hunting and Fishing Scenes, *dated 1769 in the plate, full repeat, cotton and linen, printed from two copperplates in aubergine with additional colors added by wood-block-printing and stenciling, Middlesex, England.*

13. *Bed à la polonaise hung with Jean-Baptiste Huët for Oberkampf Manuf.,* L'Abreuvoir *(The Horse Pond), 1796-97.*

14. *Window dressing (curtains, pelmet, and tiebacks) with Jean-Baptiste Huët for Oberkampf Manuf.,* Les Quatre Parties du monde *(The Four Continents), c. 1792-94.*

aspects of life—history, current events, literature, and popular culture—that had previously been recorded in engravings on paper suddenly began appearing on cloth as well. At first the designs were produced in shades of red, using madder dyes, or indigo blue on white or off-white backgrounds. In a few deluxe examples, additional colors were printed with wood blocks or painted in by hand **(fig. 12)**. (Chemical advances of the early nineteenth century would expand the color range to include purple, black, green, and ochre.) Building on the precedent of a room decorated with charming *indiennes* (calicoes) by

Louis XV's mistress, Madame de Pompadour, and later, another by Catherine the Great of Russia,[9] it became the vogue in the late eighteenth century to do up entire rooms with all manner of narrative toile pictures. Printed on cotton, or a cotton and linen blend, pictorial fabric covered the walls, upholstered the furniture, and draped the windows and bed **(fig. 13-14)**.

The first known English yardage that is signed and dated, a pastoral setting with peacocks and poultry amid antique ruins, was printed by Robert Jones in 1761, the year he opened his factory at Old Ford, east of London on the River Lea in Middlesex **(fig. 15)**.

From surviving artifacts, we know that French manufacturers produced at least one version of his design, of course without his signature.[10] In general, the refined beauty of the English designs and the outstanding quality of their engraving and printing dominated the early playing field in the 1750s through the 1770s, and so it is not surprising that the French, as they began to develop a copperplate-printed textile industry of their own, should imitate the best of British production. Indeed, in the absence of English copyright laws before 1787, some of the most desired designs were produced in both countries. (And later, when certain English firms went out of business because of domestic and Continental pirating, wood blocks and copperplates doubtless made their way across the Channel into France.)

In the 1770s, however, while British printed cottons were still unsurpassed, a budding manufacturer in France named Christophe-Philippe Oberkampf (1738-1815) began making frequent reconnaissance trips to England, where he had some designs printed and where he collected examples of English prints from which to copy and learn. At Old Ford he succeeded in hiring a principal designer (a Swiss Protestant like himself) away from Robert Jones. Oberkampf would soon become England's biggest rival in the business. Having been raised in a family of textile dyers, he was thoroughly trained in all aspects of the business when he arrived in Paris from Basel in 1758, just as the seventy-three-year ban on the import, production, and even the wearing of printed cotton was being repealed.[11] Of the textile manufac-

15. *Detail of Robert Jones, Old Ford Manuf., Old Ford Pastorale, dated 1761 in the plate. This example of an early English copperplate design was printed from the firm's—and the printed textile industry's—first signed and dated plate (to the right of the chicks).*

16. *J.P. Meillier Manuf., detail of* Diane et Endymion, *c.1792, Beautiran, France.*

The Wild-Duck, hence,
O'er the rough Moss, and o'er
  the trackless Waste
The heath-Hen flutters,
  (pious Fraud!) to lead
The hot pursuing Spaniel far astray
James Thomson "Spring" The Seasons

17. *Oberkampf Manuf., detail of* Jeu d'enfants *(Children's Games), 1770-1783.*

tories established in France in the 1760s, his firm at the village of Jouy-en-Josas ultimately achieved such international acclaim that all printed textiles, regardless of their place of manufacture, came to be known generically as *toiles-de-Jouy*. Today, they are still referred to that way, or even more inaccurately as "toiles" (a French word for plain-woven, unadorned, canvas-type material).

In addition to having practical experience, the young Oberkampf already embodied other essential qualities necessary to succeed; he was shrewd, a perfectionist, and driven; he possessed an unfailing sense of good design and an uncanny intuition for presenting timely subjects. Oberkampf was also a highly moral and fair, if demanding, employer whose diplomacy and understanding of subtle politics would prove invaluable throughout the long political turmoil following the French Revolution. But at the outset, his plant was optimally located to satisfy the physical demands of his textile-printing business (an abundant, clean water supply), as well as the need for a rich marketing arena (proximity to the royal palace at Versailles). As Oberkampf was setting up his initial production line to print woodblock patterns for dress

goods (which would always comprise the larger part of his yardage and profits), he was also secretly developing improved copperplate technology: a new version of an intaglio press for printing engravings on yardage for clothing and furnishing. By 1770, the new machine was operating (see Appendix). Meanwhile, throughout this formative period, Oberkampf's younger brother was keeping abreast of developments in textile-printing establishments in Switzerland and Alsace.

Since the first civilizations, spring has been a time to celebrate new life **(figs. 15- 16)**. It is the season of nest-building, chicks hatching, and children's carefree games on tender grass sprouting around budding trees. Perhaps it was no coincidence that one of Oberkampf's earliest copperplate designs portrays children at play **(fig. 17)**. Here, the designer's particular manner of rendering the figures, connecting their games and emphasizing their diminutive scale with oversized fruit and foliage, is characteristic of a decidedly English decorative style. In fact, the design might easily be mistaken for a British production if it were not for surviving examples stamped with the earliest mark of the factory at Jouy-en-Josas **(fig. 18)**.

18. *Factory mark on an example of* Jeu d'enfants *(fig. 17). From 1760 French law required manufacturers to mark bolt ends with their firm's name, location, and the print's dye type—*bon *or* petit teint *(fast or fugitive); optional stamps were often added for inventory purposes. These* chefs-de-pièce *help us determine where and when a design was manufactured, but were often cut off in finishing.*

19. Oberkampf Manuf., Les Tuileries *or* Scènes galantes *(The Tuileries Gardens), after 1776.*

23

20. Detail of children in fig. 19.

21. Carl Guttenberg after Moreau le Jeune, Rendez-vous pour Marly *(Outing at the Royal Park of Marly), 1776, engraving on paper for* L'Histoire du costume en France dans le dix-huitième siècle, *a Parisian journal compiled and reissued as* Monument du costume.

The adults of the eighteenth century were no less eager than those of today to get out of doors in the first gentle weather of spring and, in their case, to parade the latest bonnets and clothing styles. Here again, the most enterprising players to recognize an opportunity and turn it to their advantage were Protestant émigrés from Switzerland. At the same time that some of them were reentering France to build the industry for printed cotton dress goods, others, working with these manufacturers, transformed the larger marketing picture by developing the early prototypes of today's fashion magazines. Suddenly, copperplate designs printed on yardage intended for home furnishing were displaying some of the same fashion models who appeared in the illustrations for these trendy periodicals—some of them wearing dresses made from *toiles-de-Jouy*.

A good example of the interchange between fashion illustration and printed fabric is provided by a pair of children seen playing with a drum in one of Oberkampf's textiles known as *The Tuileries* (the royal gardens adjacent to the Louvre and a favorite place to promenade the latest fashions; **(figs. 19-20)**. His designer copied the children from an engraving dated 1776 in one of the issues of *Monument du Costume* **(fig. 21)**. But both the fashion plate and its toile counterpart are interesting in yet another sense—one that admirably demonstrates how closely prints on paper and their cloth cousins tended to reflect aspects of their time and culture. To eighteenth-century consumers, the unusually relaxed, informal way the chil-

22. Detail of Oberkampf Manuf., Le Tombeau de Jean-Jacques Rousseau *(The Tomb of Jean-Jacques Rousseau), 1778 or after.*

dren are dressed immediately conveyed their newly found freedom. An association would have been made with the controversial theories that the philosopher Jean-Jacques Rousseau (1712-1778) had been exploring in his popular novels, such as treating children as reasoning individuals entitled to their own inclinations. His wide following would have immediately connected the visual reference to an episode in *The New Heloise*, 1761: the theft of a child's drum by an older sibling. Rousseau did not counsel corporal punishment, but a more reasoned approach based on cause and effect (essentially, the Golden Rule), which to his detractors was heresy.[13] In addition to raising

the hot topic of children's education, a parklike setting in Oberkampf's textile would have appealed to gardening fans who were following the latest developments in French landscape architecture. One of its main innovators, the Marquis de Girardin (1735-1806), erected a funerary monument for Rousseau on his own property when the philosopher died at Ermenonville in 1778 during a long visit. A vista with Rousseau's tomb placed within a larger garden setting of the type advocated by Girardin, was commemorated in an engraving, which became famous immediately. Not surprisingly, the work inspired a new toile design from Oberkampf's establishment[14] **(fig. 22)**.

25

23. Summer, *from James Thomson,* The Seasons *(Perth ed., 1793), engraving by Francis Chesham after a painting by Charles Catton.*

TWO
Summer

Home, from his morning Task, the Swain retreats. . .
While the full-udder'd Mother lows around
The cheerful Cottage. . .
And, in a Corner of the buzzing Shade,
The House-Dog, with the vacant Greyhound, lies
Out-stretch'd, and sleepy. . . .

James Thomson, *"Summer,"* The Seasons

24. Detail of Frontispiece: Summer, *from* The Four Seasons *textile, after 1793.*

25. Jean-Baptiste Huët for Oberkampf
Manuf., La Couronnement de la Rosière
*(The Crowning of the Rosemaiden), 1789-
1792, full repeat. Huët may be depicting
not just any garden-variety Rosemaiden
but the specific girl who was cheated of her
award in 1774; later, she was successfully
defended by a lawyer who turned the case
into a propagandistic cause for the
Revolution (and who afterward became
President of the National Assembly).*

> With all her gay-dress'd maids
>   attending round.
> One chief, in gracious Dignity
>   inthron'd,
> Shines o're the Rest, the
>   pastoral Queen, and rays
> Her smiles, sweet-beaming,
>   on her Shepherd-King;
> While the glad Circle round them
>   yield their Souls to festive mirth.

James Thomson "Summer," The Seasons

From her adolescence, Stéphanie-Félicité Ducrest de Saint-Aubin, the future Comtesse de Genlis (1746-1830), indulged her passion for creating theatrical events. Later, as a respected educator and author and the trend-setting mistress of the duke of Orleans, she advocated Rousseau's philosophy of living a life close to nature and liked to stage her amusements in pastoral garden settings. No doubt she was inspired, like many others, by the Rousseauian landscape theories of the Marquis de Girardin. One summer, near Salency in Picardy, the countess playfully transformed a local, rural festival into a grand amusement for her noble friends. They, in turn, were not above dressing in costume and assuming the roles of shepherds and milkmaids to accommodate her imaginative entertainment, which was based on an annual summer celebration dating back to the sixth century when St. Médard honored the most beautiful and virtuous maiden in the region with a crown of roses and 250 francs **(fig. 25)**. As a result of the popularity in high society of the rustic "Rosemaiden" festival, several theatrical works were written around its theme. In the 1780s, the pleasure in bucolic masquerade reached a peak when Marie

26. Apron made of cotton printed by J. P. Meillier Manuf., Diane et Endymion, c. 1792, Beautiran, France.

27. Detail of fig. 26: Meeting.

28. Detail of fig. 26: Courtship.

Antoinette created a showcase farm, Le Hameau, on the formal grounds at Versailles and required her courtiers to dress as its denizens. As visual vestiges of this amusement, some of the love scenes printed by a textile manufacturer in Beautiran seem to encapsulate set pieces from a romantic play or novel **(figs. 26-28)**. The apron made of the textile was probably never meant for hard drudgery in some scullery; its vignettes suggest instead that it was part of a costume for an aristocratic diversion like those staged by the Queen.

Artistic practice has long associated images of summer with adolescence, exploiting the opportunities to portray the pastimes and sweet raptures of young love and courtship savored over the season's long, sultry afternoons. Having overcome initial growing pains during its first two decades, the French printed textile industry was coming into its own by the third quarter of the century. Indeed, English firms were being undermined by cheap local and Continental imitations; Robert Jones, for one, had to close his doors by 1780. The year 1783 witnessed a peace treaty between Britain and France. It was then that the King awarded the coveted designation of "Royal Manufactory" to Oberkampf's establishment at Jouy-en-Josas. The privilege signaled that France was taking over the industry's lead from Great Britain. It also marked the beginning of a business bond between the manufacturer and an exceptional artist whose superior ability to create winning toile designs over the next twenty-eight years would ensure the factory's fame.[15] That was also the year Jean-Baptiste Huët (1743-1811) prepared his first cartoon, or full-scale drawing, for Oberkampf to commemorate his factory's new royal status. The resulting textile is renowned for its information and unrivaled among *toiles-de-Jouy* for its artistry. Known as *Les Travaux de la manufacture*, or The Factory in Operation (see Fig 76 and Appendix), it integrates many sketches the artist drew on-site, and it shows all aspects of the plant and its workers in full operation.

Huët was particularly suited to creating compositions that would work well as printed textile designs. The son of the king's chief furniture painter, he was a respected member of the French Academy and a gifted animal painter who had learned first-hand from two great Rococo artists, François Boucher and Jean-Honoré Fragonard. He had also designed tapestries for the king's workshop. But most useful of all was Huët's ability as a printmaker. In the early 1770s, he had prepared many series of prints to be employed both as instructional models for drawing students and also as designs for other artists working in the decorative arts. Because he understood exactly how much labor went into engraving a copperplate, he was able to regulate the amount of time (and expense) by controlling the quantity of detail in the drawings he prepared for Oberkampf's engravers to follow. This particular tactic saved money for Oberkampf. What is more, Huët had amassed a large print collection of his own from which to borrow ideas and models. Favorite figures appear over and again in his compositions, reversed in their poses or dressed in different costumes. Nevertheless, the scenes he created never look

pieced together, nor do they exhibit the incongruities of scale of many designs by lesser toile artists. To the contrary, Huët's people and exceptionally lifelike animals always seem to move and interact with natural, easy grace in a charming ambiance unique to this artist.

This lyric grace radiates from Huët's *Les Délices des quatres saisons* (endpapers), which hymns the rewards of seasonal pastimes and labors. We can virtually smell the spring earth under cultivation and the heady fragrance of autumn's grapes, and hear the bagpipes of summer and a dog barking to his wading mistress: throw that stick now, please. Everywhere there is an easy familiarity between man and beast, young and old, as they play out the year together in lively good cheer. Who would guess that this seamless natural panorama is a pastiche of motifs from Old Master prints? Indeed, Huët mined his rich collection of engravings after Flemish and Dutch seventeenth-century paintings and mixed groups and figures to suit his seasonal theme. Elements of canvases by David Teniers (1610-1690), Philips Wouwerman (1619-1668), and less-known genre printmakers[16] lie behind this and other of his designs, and reflect the retrospective taste of his time for older Netherlandish art.

The taste was political and nostalgic, as well as commercially manipulated. Some of the restive aristocracy of France admired the social structure of seventeenth-century Holland as they yearned for a new order at home. At the same time, the current craze for Old Master Dutch and Flemish paintings and prints fed on itself, and Dutch peasants and windmills seemed to be popping up everywhere—in contemporary paintings, print collections, garden decorations, and, not least, in the images of printed textiles. As ever, *toiles-de-Jouy* reflected and helped form fashion. **31**

29. *Manuf. unknown,* Le Jardin d'amour *(The Garden of Love), c. 1790, full repeat, Nantes, France.*

30. *Detail of Jean-Baptiste Huët for Oberkampf Manuf.,* Le Parc du château *(The Palace Park), 1784-1785, fragment. The detail of Huët's boat likely served as a model for the same motif in fig. 29.*

Although the supreme reputation enjoyed by the toiles printed at Jouy-en-Josas was well deserved, the town was by no means the only center of cotton printing.[17] Most of the other European countries, and even Russia, had fabric-printing works, although very few produced scenic copperplate prints of any note, and the majority concentrated largely on woodblock prints, despite the lower productivity of that method. Well before the 1770s, other manufacturers in France, largely Swiss immigrants, had established firms around Paris, Rouen, Marseilles, and Orange, and also on the Swiss border in Alsace, which did not offi-cially become part of France until 1798. Of them all, the most prolific group of cotton printers set up shops on the bridges in the Breton port city of Nantes, which was a main hub for the slave trade.[18] Light, bright, washable printed cottons were one of the prime exports of Nantes, to be exchanged in Africa for slaves and in the West Indies for coffee, sugar, and spices. Despite the Nantes printers' prosperity, they did not challenge Oberkampf's dominance: the boat motif in **figure 29** derives from that in Huët's earlier design, **figure 30**, typifying the greater creativity at Jouy-en-Josas.

33

As for Huët himself, under Oberkampf's direction he was the one largely responsible for the stylistic evolution of Jouy's textile designs over the years, as witnessed by the changes in the firm's depiction of children and animals. When compared with Huët's goat-cart motif of about 1800 **(fig. 32)**, the dog-drawn cart in Oberkampf's very early *Jeu d'enfants* **(fig. 31)** looks somewhat awkwardly sketched, and its stylized silhouette defines a limited space that belies the childrens' playful energy. The young bird-catcher and dancing boys on one of Huët's last textiles designs **(fig. 33)**, on the other hand, interact freely in multi-layered vignettes that somehow seem believable, despite the artificial pattern of the background.

31. *Detail of a dog cart, a motif in the textile pattern shown in part in fig. 17.*

32. *Detail of Jean-Baptiste Huët for Oberkampf Manuf., Les Plaisirs du campagne (Country Pleasures, also known as The Stag Hunt), c. 1800, engraved roller-printed cotton.*

33. *Jean-Baptiste Huët for Oberkampf Manuf.,* L'Oiseleur *(The Bird Catcher), 1811, engraved roller-printed cotton, full repeat. This potent allegorical motif for the young bird thief (the sexual imagery had political implications) was based on a tapestry design Boucher made for the Beauvais workshop, for which Huët also created designs in the early 1780s.*

> By tyrant Man
> Inhuman caught, and in the narrow Cage
> From Liberty confined
> > *James Thomson "Spring,"* The Seasons

35

34. Autumn, *from James Thomson,* The Seasons *(Perth ed., 1793), engraving by Francis Chesham after a painting by Richard Corbould.*

THREE
Autumn

Before the ripen'd Field the Reapers stand,
In fair Array.
At once they stoop and swell the lusty Sheaves. . .
The Breath of Orchard big with bending Fruit. . .

. . . .

Think, oh grateful, think!
How good the God of Harvest is to you;
Who pours Abundance o'er your flowing Fields.

James Thomson, "Autumn," The Seasons

35. *Detail of Frontispiece:* Autumn, *from* The Four Seasons *textile, after 1793, English.*

36. *Manuf. unknown, harvesting scenes from a textile depicting an autumn courtship, 1790s, full repeat, England. Not only is there a common source for the background grain-harvesting scene here, and for fig. 35 and the Frontispiece, but other stylistic similarities between these two textiles suggest that they may have been produced by the same manufacturer.*

Old orders fall and fortunes change. The peasant maiden in **figure 36**, a British fabric, is wooed and won by a gentleman. In France, Louis XVI swears to uphold the constitution while new citoyens dance on the ruins of the Bastille in a toile commemorating the first anniversary of the Republic **(fig. 37)**. Produced on the brink of the Revolution, one airy cotton design from Nantes anticipated the radical transformation of mood and style that would prevail after the monarchy was ousted in 1789 **(fig. 38)**. While the peaceful landscape printed on this *toile-de-Nantes* appears to mirror the contemporary French countryside and the traditional fall custom of hunting, the women pursuing a stag with bows and arrows, horns and hounds, and the ancient goddess Diana and her nymphs, clearly illustrate Greek and Roman mythology. The cameolike medallions punctuating the pattern augur a trend, begun earlier in British architecture, that would transform not only the look of French fabrics for home décor, but the fashion for accessories as well. A comparable, if somewhat later, toile design by Huët from Jouy-en-Josas reflects conflicting sentiments of nostalgia and eagerness for change **(fig. 39)**. Nodding to Neoclassical taste, the goddess of Fortune is seen seated within a symbolic wheel of

37. *Detail of Jean-Baptiste Huët for Oberkampf Manuf.,* La Fête de la féderation (*Celebration of the Federation, July 14, 1790*), *1790-1791. Commemorating the Revolution's first anniversary and the new constitutional monarchy, this design shows representatives from France's départements, which replaced the old provinces; Louis XVI swears an oath to the new nation, while Marie Antoinette looks on from below, and citizens dance on the ruins of the Bastille.*

39

38. Manuf. unknown, Diane, *c. 1785, full repeat, Nantes, France.*

39. Detail of Jean-Baptiste Huët for Oberkampf Manuf., Fontaine et animaux *(Fountain and Animals), c. 1803. The goddess is seated among pastoral design elements favored by the deposed absolutist regime, but she turns the wheel of fortune, a reference to the cataclysmic changes in the power structure of Europe in the late eighteenth century.*

40

40. *Dubern or Dubey. Manuf.,* La Chasse de Diane *(Diana at the Hunt), either c. 1790 or c. 1810 (see note 19), Nantes, France. The man-faced stag is the hunter Acteon, transformed in punishment for having spied on the bathing Diana and comically illustrating the price of ignoring the warning "Never fool Mother Nature."*

41. *Petitpierre Manuf.,* Diane Chasseresse *(Diana the huntress), c. 1800, detail with factory mark, Nantes, France. This Nantes textile is a copy of one Huët designed for Oberkampf c. 1798, which appears on the bed in fig. 1.*

fortune. Yet this medallion motif supports a Rococo-style fountain flanked by a peacock and assorted birds fully reminiscent of the first toile design produced at Old Ford nearly half a century before.

A Nantes factory founded in 1780 by a calico dealer named Pierre Dubern continued to popularize legends about Diana with renditions of her adventures with the Caledonian Boar and the ill-starred hunter, Acteon **(fig. 40)**.[19] And in further tribute to her, around the turn of the century, the Petitpierre brothers of Nantes brought out a close, but somewhat less graceful, reversed copy of a *toile-de-Jouy* that had been designed by Huët and featured Diana as the huntress **(fig. 41)**. France had been in love with this goddess for centuries, ever since she dominated the decorative scheme in the Renaissance chateau of Francis I at Fontainebleau. By the eighteenth century, a famous antique marble statue of Diana in her role

as huntress had been moved from that country chateau to Versailles; by 1798, it was placed on public view at the Louvre. Considered one of France's great treasures, it was a prime model for many artworks, and Huët's *Diane chasseresse* toile design for Oberkampf **(fig. 1)** was one of them.

More generally, the discoveries of Pompeii and Herculaneum in the 1740s, and ongoing archaeological explorations in those ancient cities, led to a renewed fascination with classical art and literature. The associations of Pompeiian classicism with Republican Rome made the style appealing to the revolutionaries, who sought a new iconography of power. That British antiquarians and artists such as the Adam brothers were early in shaping Neoclassicism did not discourage French imitations and adaptations.[20] Then, during his extraordinary rise to power and his grand emulation of imperial Rome at the turn of the century, Napoleon Bonaparte carried these ideas even further. Toile design, with the rest of fashion, turned Neoclassical to support his imperial pose.

Many archaeological artifacts were carefully documented in engravings, not only to satisfy the public's insatiable curiosity about the subject, but also to record and promote the rapidly growing collections of antiquities in private hands. In some cases, published albums of such collections, including engravings with detailed descriptions, doubled as sales catalogues and functioned as marketing devices as well as educational tools. As with the apparel industry, printed textile manufacturers worked hand in glove with engravers and print sellers for everyone's mutual profit.

In the post-revolutionary era, French manufacturers were swift to embrace Neoclassicism. As they began catering to this vogue, they sought to reflect ancient domestic interiors, many of which were revealed intact by the continuing excavations. Their designers recreated the ornamental decorations they observed in fanciful antique wall paintings, sculpture, and carved gemstones (or cameos), with their encyclopedic store of mythological motifs. Huët had special access to such sources. Having grown up in his father's apartment in the Louvre, and privileged to have his own quarters in that palace until 1802, he was able to inspect firsthand the royal collection of antiquities and the publications of other collections. (The grand palace had been the home and government seat of Louis XVI until his imprisonment and execution in 1792. Thereafter it was declared a national museum; the royal library, which included an extensive collection of prints, began admitting the public in 1791.)

Oberkampf wrote to Huët in 1799 that he wanted to respond to the growing vogue for the antique style of the "cameo"—or what he termed the "lozenge"—and Huët complied with a rash of drawings in the new style. Nonetheless, this invincible team of artist and manufacturer continued to produce some designs conceived in their older, pastoral style (no doubt to satisfy clients clinging to the tradition). Only now, there was often a remarkable technical difference in the textiles they produced. Their *Stag Hunt* of about 1800 is a triumphant example of an old-fashioned design produced with the cutting-edge technology of engraved roller printing **(fig. 32)**.[21] This was a process that had been developed in 1783 by the Scotsman, Thomas Bell, but its use in Britain had been limited to small dress patterns. By 1797, Oberkampf's nephew and scientific collaborator, the chemist Samuel Widmer, had built France's first continuous-printing roller machine at Jouy. And although the relatively small diameter of its engraved copper roller made it necessary to reduce the vertical design repeat of scenic patterns by half (to roughly twenty inches), the gain in a single day's printing production was enormous.

To maximize production from all his operating facilities, Oberkampf continued to make plate-printed cottons, some of them with smaller vertical repeats that were comparable in size to those of the new engraved roller textiles **(fig. 42)**.[22] In 1805, Napoleon visited Jouy-en-Josas to honor the distinguished, naturalized French citizen with a personal tour of the factory. In 1806, Oberkampf was awarded the Legion of Honor and a First Class Gold Medal for his pioneering role in the development of the printed textile industry in France. And in 1810, his nephew Widmer again brought honor to the family firm when he won the Grand Decennial Prize for his formula for a solid green that was colorfast and could be printed with a double

42. *Detail of Jean-Baptiste Huët for Oberkampf Manuf.,* Les Losanges *(Emblems of the Harvest), c. 1800, Jouy-en-Josas, France. Huët adapted figures and the diamond grid from antique sources, many known through the eight-volume* Le pitture antiche d'Ercolano e contorni, *1757-1792, which reproduces engravings of finds at Herculaneum. This influential publication, produced by the Royal Herculaneum Academy, was widely circulated in Europe among aristocratic connoisseurs.*

dye in a single operation. (Formerly, greens were printed in a labor-intensive two-step overlay process.) Naturally, Oberkampf brought out the first textile printed in green with the efficient new technology.[23]

The entrepreneur was well aware that Napoleon's tastes were not restricted to one vision of antiquity. Responsive to the court's wide-ranging antiquarianism, Huët and his contemporaries also combed Renaissance books of design and accounts of earlier archaeological discoveries for models and ideas. They borrowed from the work of sixteenth-century artists, who had similarly mined the archeological excavations of their time and conveyed their findings through their art. One of the most famous examples is the series of wall paintings that Raphael began in 1516 at the Vatican. His ambitious interior decoration project was substantially inspired by the Golden House of the Roman emperor Nero, which had been built in the first century A.D. Copied in prints many times during the sixteenth and seventeenth centuries, Raphael's compositions became widely known to the eighteenth century through meticulous engravings in lavish serial publications, which became a major source for the Neoclassical style **(figs. 43-45)**.[24]

According to some accounts, Oberkampf's bedroom was decorated at one point with a toile-de-Jouy of numerous motifs borrowed from Raphael.[25] Could the toile have been a design that Huët drew around 1806 for a roller engraving of squirrels, sphinxes, butterflies, and pairs of grape-picking cherubs borrowed directly from the Vatican paintings **(fig. 46)**? This toile pattern is not conceived in the tightly compartmentalized, cameo style characteristic of many Neoclassical textiles, and its creatures look so natural that one might assume the gifted animal painter drew them directly from life.

If some of Oberkampf's Neoclassical yardage appears to have been printed directly from antique cameos, the illusion was calculated. In the decade following the French Revolution, some Parisian printmaking establishments, notably the one founded before 1772 by an Englishman known as Arthur, reorganized to produce highly refined etched plates in a variety of shapes and sizes. To recreate the effect of gems carved in relief, they combined many intaglio techniques, particularly the new, tonal process of aquatint, in which powdered resin is melted on the plate before it is immersed in acid. The result when inked and printed is a velvety dark background that visually recedes behind the lighter motifs worked against it. The designers appropriated ornaments and mythological motifs from antique sources and surrounded them with etched or engraved decorative frames. The plates could be printed to order on a wide range of materials: from ordinary paper intended for antiquarians, collectors, and book illustrations to hand-tinted papers meant to be cut out and applied in various decorative arrangements on a wall—a type of collaged wallpaper known as *papier-en-feuilles*. In addition, intaglio medallions, lozenges, and borders graced silk sashes and ribbons **(figs. 47-48),** purses, window shades, and men's waistcoats **(figs. 49-50)**; and tiny plates might be printed on paper or cloth, cut out, glazed, and framed for use as buttons or brooches **(figs. 51-52)**, or mounted and varnished to decorate snuffboxes or board games.[26]

Somewhat larger prints, like the ones seen in **figures 53** and **54**, could be used to ornament upholstered furniture. In 1791, the printmaker Jean-Baptiste Lucien (1748-1806) combined techniques of line etching, aquatint, and stipple to reproduce allegorical bas-reliefs that the sculptor Jean-Guillaume

45

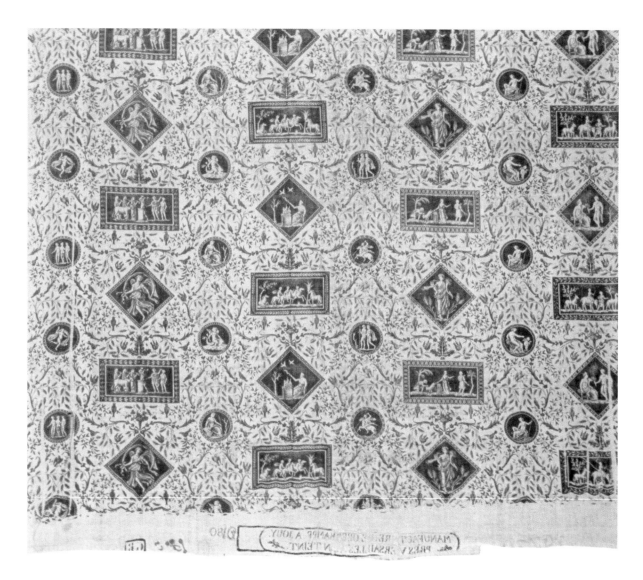

43. *Oberkampf Manuf., Les Oiseaux (The Birds), 1790s, full repeat with factory mark.*

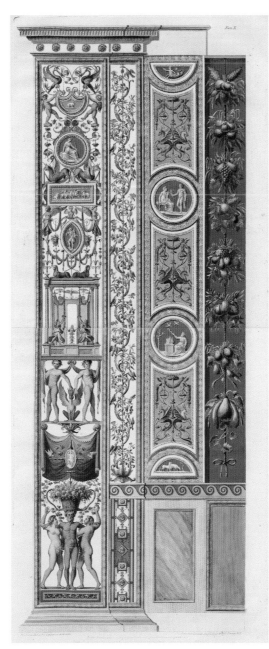

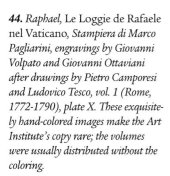

44. *Raphael,* Le Loggie de Rafaele nel Vaticano, *Stampiera di Marco Pagliarini, engravings by Giovanni Volpato and Giovanni Ottaviani after drawings by Pietro Camporesi and Ludovico Tesco, vol. 1 (Rome, 1772-1790), plate X. These exquisitely hand-colored images make the Art Institute's copy rare; the volumes were usually distributed without the coloring.*

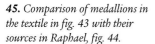

45. *Comparison of medallions in the textile in fig. 43 with their sources in Raphael, fig. 44.*

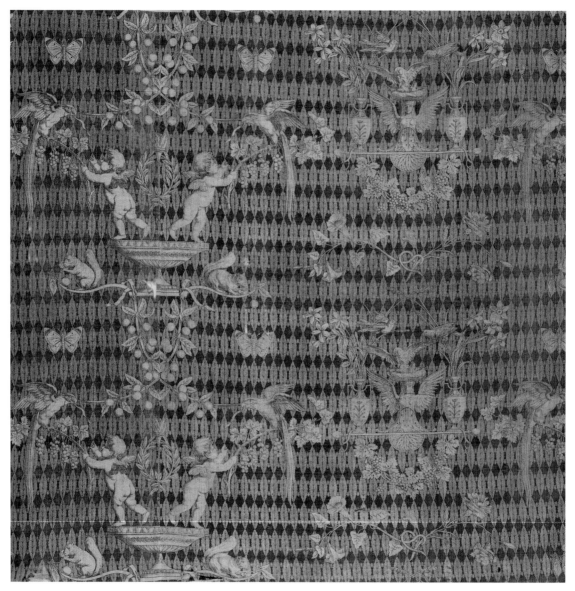

46. *Jean-Baptiste Huët for Oberkampf Manuf.,* Oiseaux et écureuils *(Birds and Squirrels), 1805-1806, full repeat, engraved roller-printed cotton. Although this design celebrating the autumn harvest recalls Huët's earlier, pastoral mode, it is nevertheless based on some of the same antique motifs that Raphael appropriated for his wall paintings in the Vatican.*

47. Oberkampf Manuf., border print with antique-inspired medallions, c. 1795. This is one of Oberkampf's versions of the medallion border prints produced in Paris during the 1790s by specialty print workshops; these were intended to decorate accessories and domestic interiors.

Moitte (1746-1810) designed to celebrate the transition in the French government to a constitutional monarchy. The prints record friezes on a temporary triumphal arch erected on the Champ de Mars in Paris, and while impressions have survived on paper, this unusual appearance on silk may be unique. But the value of the two examples in the collection of the Allentown Art Museum extends beyond their rarity: Moitte was not just the relief sculptor but also a principal designer for the multipurpose plates produced by

Arthur's firm. Given that all of his friezes were recorded in prints, it is conceivable that they may all have ended up displayed together on a handsome set of chairs. It is amusing to think of a soft, padded chair back upholstered in a fabric printed to resemble a stone relief. Evidently, while fashion required decoration *à l'antique*, comfort still required modern stuffing.

The richness of Neoclassicism inspired diverse forms of artistry, while the turmoil accompanying the French Revolution led some artists to flee Paris to

48. Manuf. unknown, silk ribbon printed with Revolutionary medallions and slogans, 1790s, Paris(?), France. At the first anniversary of the Revolution, July 14, 1790 (see fig. 37), some 300,000 people assembled in Paris, all wearing such ribbons (according to an eyewitness report in the journal Révolutions de Paris, *July 17, 1790).*

49

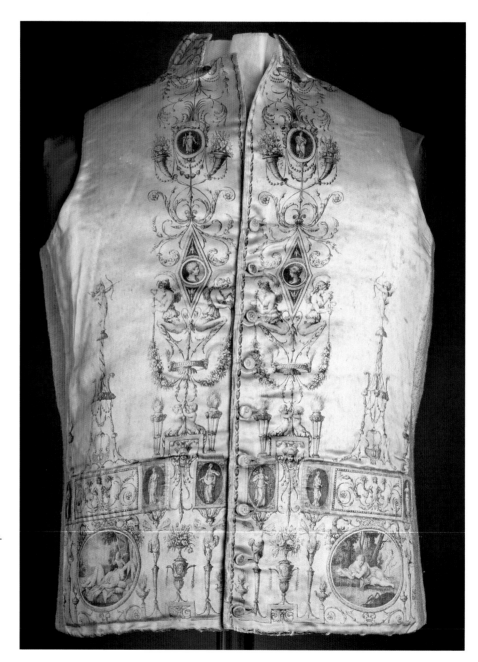

49. *Robert et Cie., Manuf., man's waistcoat, 1795, copper-plate-printed silk satin front, linen back, Paris, France. The intricate design comprises arabesques, grotesques, and medallions framing Narcissus and another mythological figure.*

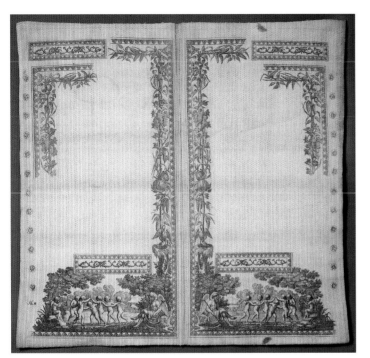

50. *Manuf. unknown, untailored waistcoat, including button coverings, 1795, white ribbed cotton copperplate-printed in green, Paris(?) France. The corn, grapes, pears, and pumpkins in the borders represent the autumn harvest, while Father Time, watching children dance, reminds us of the passage of time and the succession of generations.*

51. *Attributed to Baron Dominique Vivant Denon (1747-1825), portrait medallions for prints, c. 1793, (see fig. 52), pen and ink with washes. An observant artist, as well as an astute collector, writer, and diplomat, Vivant Denon may be best known as an archaeologist who accompanied Napoleon on his Egyptian campaign, and as France's first director-general of museums (including the Louvre).*

52. *Jean-Baptiste Morret (or Moret; print publisher active in Paris, 1790-1820), sheet with thirty portrait medallions, 1790s, Paris, France, etching, aquatint, hand-painted and printed in colors. In the 1790s, sheets of miniature portraits appeared in fashion magazines to display the latest hat designs and hairstyles; small, printed medallions like these were also designed to be printed on silk, cotton, or paper to decorate snuff boxes, wallpaper, clothing, and accessories. A glazing technique for buttons, securing tiny pictures under glass, was patented in England in 1774.*

53. *Jean-Baptiste Lucien after Jean-Guillaume Moitte, for Arthur & Robert Manuf.(?),* Nous ne vous craindrons plus, subalternes tirans, vous qui nous opprimés sous cents noms diférens *(We do not fear you, infernal tyrants . . .), copperplate print on silk satin for chair covering, 1791, Paris, France. This allegory of the liberation of the Bastille, based partly on the Parthenon friezes, shows the aristocracy crushed beneath the toppling prison, while Liberty, with her sword and Phrygian cap, tramples a hydra symbolizing the* ancien regime.

54. *Jean-Baptiste Lucien after Jean-Guillaume Moitte, for Arthur & Robert Manuf.(?),* La Patrie *(France under the new constitution)* with Vous chérissez cette liberté. Vous la possédez maintenant. Montrez vous digne de la conserver *(Cherish and protect your new liberty . . .), copperplate print on silk satin for chair covering, 1791. At left, the allegorical figure of La Patrie, identified by her crown and olive branch, leads the Royal Family, followed by a group of legislators and* citoyens, *who are kept in order by a soldier, at right, wearing armor* à l'antique.

53

55. *Marie-Bonaventure Lebert for Hartmann et fils in assoc. with Soehnée l'Aîné et Cie.,* Spring and Summer, *cartoon for* Allegory of the Four Seasons *textile, 1806-1807, pen and brown ink, brush and grey wash squared in graphite for transfer, on four sheets of paper, pasted together, Munster, France. Above, Flora, symbolizing Spring, is kissed by the wind god Zephyr, while a river god slumbers beneath them and children lead sheep to pasture. Below, the enthroned Summer goddess Ceres receives offerings of grain and fruit in thanks for the fertility of field and womb, while distant dancers rejoice amid waving wheat.*

56. *Marie-Bonaventure Lebert for Hartmann et fils in assoc. with Soehnée l'Ainé et Cie.,* Allegory of the Four Seasons, *c. 1807(?), copperplate-printed textile, Munster, France.*

57. Marie-Bonaventure Lebert for Hartmann et fils in assoc. with Soehnée l'Ainé et Cie., Autumn and Winter, *cartoon for* Allegory of the Four Seasons *textile, 1806-1807, pen and brown ink, brush and grey wash squared in graphite for transfer, on four sheets of paper, pasted together. Above, the tipsy Bacchus toasts the Autumn harvest, while merrymakers draw him toward an altar where Silenus makes a sacrifice of thanksgiving. Below, Chronos, or Father Time, warms himself and his sleepy bear before a cave; a party at the left is picnicking, seemingly indifferent to Winter.*

55

58. *Marie-Bonaventure Lebert for Hartmann et fils in assoc. with Soehnée l'Ainé et Cie.,* Les Eléments *(The Four Elements with Zodiac Bands) 1818 or earlier, Munster, France.*

[on the elements:]
By Nature's all-refining Hand prepar'd
Of temper'd Sun, and Water, Earth, and Air,
In ever-changing Composition mixt.
   James Thomson "Autumn," The Seasons

[on the zodiac:]
But who can count the stars of Heaven?
Who sing their Influence on this lower world?..
The nightly sky,
And all her glowing Constellations pour
Their rigid influence down.
   James Thomson "Winter," The Seasons

59. *Jean-Baptiste Huët for Oberkampf Manuf.,* Medallions et Cartouches à l'antique *(Medallions and cartouches in antique style with the four elements), 1800-1805. Surrounded by fruits of the harvest and vintage, medallion figures symbolize the elements: a Nereid holding a fish (Water) faces Minerva holding an owl (Air); the head of winged Mercury between birds reiterates the theme; an altar with a burning lamp stands for Fire; above and beneath it, Earth is represented by a serpent slithering below an ox used for plowing fields.*

60. *Detail of Jean-Jacques Lagrené for Oberkampf Manuf.,* Les Quatre Éléments *(The Four Elements), 1783-1789, based on engravings by Charles Depuis (1685-1742) and Louis Desplaces (1682-1739) after paintings by Louis de Boullonge le Jeune (1654-1733, Jouy-en-Josas, France. The engravings Lagrené used were made between 1717 and 1721. Shown here is Water portrayed as "The Triumph of Neptune and Amphitrite."*

57

62

61-66. Marie-Bonaventure Lebert, developmental studies for the textile reproduced in fig. 58, Les Eléments, *manufactured before 1818. These five drawings in pen and ink, on paper, some with wash added, were executed for Hartmann et fils in assoc. with Soehnée l'Aîné et Cie., Munster, France.* **61.** *An alternative design, with ornate arabesques and non-zodiac borders, this early idea was ultimately rejected;* **62.** *Detail of an alternative idea, with figures surrounded by an ornate framework and careful working of the Zodiac scheme in the vertical bands;* **63.** *A transitional drawing for the final design of Les Eléments, before the addition of Zodiac motifs in the decorative bands;* **64.** *Detail of a transitional study for* Les Eléments *showing the allegorical figures of Juno, Vulcan, Venus, and Saturn, with line drawing of Zodiac motifs.* **65.** *Study for the figures of Juno and Vulcan in* Les Eléments, *with first indications of wash modeling and the beginning of a darkened background in the Zodiac bands;* **66.** *Highly finished cartoon for the figures of Saturn and Venus as they appear in the definitive version of the design.*

find haven with provincial manufacturers. One of these artists was Marie-Bonaventure Lebert (1759-1836), who trained in the influential circle of Joseph Vien (1716-1809), the teacher of the renowned painter of Neoclassical subjects, Jacques-Louis David (1748-1815). In 1784, Lebert went to Alsace to work for the manufacturer Pierre Dollfus. Four years later he was back in Paris directing one of the specialty print workshops, but he returned to the Alsace textile-printing business after the Revolution broke out. By 1796 he had become the chief designer for Hartmann in Munster. Hartmann's firm, like that of Dollfus, was run by offspring of the founders of Mulhouse's first printed textile concern. (Like many others, its company name, and subsequently its factory marks, kept changing to reflect the succession of its partners.) We are exceptionally fortunate that a number of the textile designs produced by Lebert have been preserved at Cooper-Hewitt, the Smithsonian Institution's National Design Museum in New York. Lebert's studies and cartoons, when viewed among that museum's larger holdings of works by his peers, provide an intimate revelation of the artistic mind and hand of an accomplished textile designer. While changing currents of style are reflected in his conceptions, Lebert's drawings also show that he remained somewhat apart from the mainstream, retaining in his work—as did Huët—many

59

63

64

60

65

66

of the sweeter, more wistful sentiments of pre-revolutionary France.

Two of Lebert's drawings at Cooper-Hewitt are cartoons of 1806-1807 for a textile design that represents the Four Seasons with pastoral allegories based on ancient mythology. Rendered in pen and ink and brown wash, one sheet is overdrawn in part with a penciled grid typically used by artists to facilitate the transfer of their compositions to copperplates **(figs. 55** and **57)**. The related textile characteristically appears in a mirror image of its model **(fig. 56)**.[27]

Another series of drawings at Cooper-Hewitt **(figs. 61-66)** is related to a printed textile known as *Les Quatre Eléments* (The Four Elements; **fig. 58)**, designed for the Hartmann firm;[28] and this set has been variously attributed to Jean-François Grosjean or the younger Lebert brother. But identity in style, and annotations on one of them, support attribution to the older master. Indeed, the characteristic hand in the six related studies and cartoons could belong to no one else, and they, too, may well have been drawn in the first decade of the nineteenth century.

Some three decades earlier, Oberkampf had thrown down the gauntlet for this subject—possibly before Huët joined his ranks—by commissioning a textile design with allegorical representations of the Elements based on early eighteenth-century engravings after paintings by Louis de Boullongne (1654-1733; **fig. 60)**. With their dominant decorative frames surrounding the scenes, Lebert's first two drawings **(figs. 61-62)** for the Hartmann textile seem oddly closer in concept to this early Jouy design. One would expect them to be stylistically closer to the more contemporary design Oberkampf commissioned from Huët about 1800-1805 **(fig. 59)**, but Lebert's sensibility was obviously more retrospective. Nevertheless,

Lebert's six textile drawings depicting the Elements at Cooper-Hewitt are rare in their revelation of a designer's thought process. Huët's cartoons for Oberkampf, by contrast, are mostly all highly finished **(fig. 9**, for example) and give us little opportunity, beyond a few corrections visible on some of the sheets, to observe the artist's exploration of his subject. Huët's concept of an allegory of the Four Elements for Oberkampf provides another classic example of his crystalline antique cameo style, gently enlivened with his beloved farm animals—a signature combination in accord with the sensibility of James Thomson's *Seasons*.

Like the poet, Marie-Bonaventure Lebert also was fascinated by the ties among the Seasons, the Elements, and the stars and planets of the Zodiac. **Figures 61-62** reveal how this artist began developing his subject. These two drawings were evidently his first ideas; they included personifications of the Four Elements as mythological deities, much as they would appear in the final version, but here they are overwhelmed by an ornate, Rococo-style ornamental framework that displays related elemental and seasonal attributes. Saturn (his name designated in an inscription on one of Lebert's drawings, but confusingly identified in the museum's records as Jupiter), with cornupcopias, sits in as Earth, while a pair of dolphins frolicking in the arabesque around Venus represent Water. With her pet peacocks Juno represents Air, and Vulcan typically personifies Fire as he works at his fiery forge. Narrower bands containing signs of the Zodiac separate the panels with the gods and goddesses. But if we compare **figures 61-62** with the textile **(fig. 58)** and Lebert's subsequent drawings, it becomes evident that either he—or the manufacturer—must have rejected his first interpretation. **Figures 63-66** show his stages in revising and simplifying the design to give its themes more direct impact.

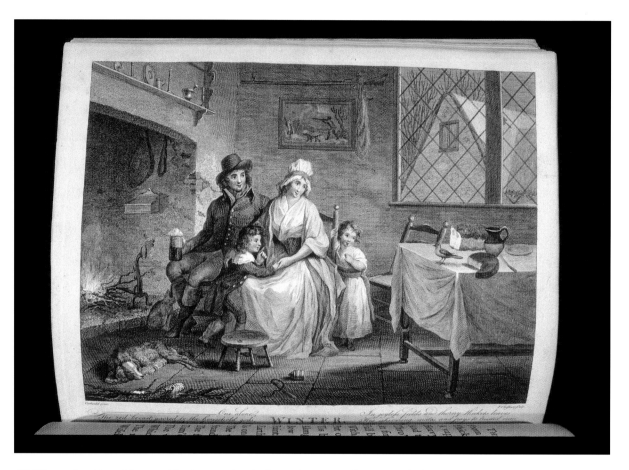

67. Winter, *from James Thomson,* The Seasons *(Perth ed., 1793), engraving by Francis Chesham after a painting by Richard Corbould.*

FOUR
Winter

Now, fond Man!
Behold thy pictur'd Life: pass some few Years,
Thy flow'ring Spring, thy short-liv'd Summer's Strength,
Thy sober Autumn, fading into Age,
And pale, concluding, Winter shuts thy Scene,
And shrouds Thee in the Grave

James Thomson, "Winter," The Seasons

68. Detail of Frontispiece: Winter, *from* The Four Seasons *textile, after 1793.*

69. *Detail of Favre Petitpierre et Cie Manuf.,* Mademoiselle de la Vallière et Louis XIV, *c. 1815, based on engravings by Louis-Charles Ruotte, fils (1754-1803), and Jean Prud'hon, fils (b. 1778), after Jean-Fréderic Schall (1752-1825), Nantes, France. This textile design is adapted from four of a series of six engravings that Ruotte and Prud'hon made from color drawings prepared by Schall, which the painter subsequently turned into popular canvases.*

The year 1815 marked the death of Christophe-Philippe Oberkampf, four years after that of Jean-Baptiste Huët. Although the manufacturer's heirs continued to commission designs from notable artists—Horace Vernet (1789-1863) and Louis-Hippolyte Le Bas (1782-1867) among them—they were unable to maintain the standards set by the firm's legendary founder. The company, ultimately under the name of Barbet de Jouy et Cie, closed in 1843 and was liquidated in 1845, and some of the blocks, plates, engraved rollers, and design archives were purchased by the Paris house of Demy-Doineau in collaboration with Braquenié. The brilliant, defining moment for figurative, copperplate-printed toiles had passed with the partners who put the tiny village of Jouy-en-Josas on the map of textile history.[29]

The year 1815 also witnessed a significant political transition with the end of the First Empire. Twice defeated, Napoleon had been banished, and France,

much weakened, had nearly shrunk back to her pre-revolutionary boundaries as the old Bourbon dynasty was returned to the throne. It was an unstable time, and the country was suffering. But the debut of a new printed textile design seemed to offer a ray of hope to the industry. Its imagery was based on an old story about an earlier Bourbon reign, revived in a novel of 1804 by the indefatigable Madame de Genlis **(fig. 69)**. Her ever-evolving writing seemed to anticipate change, if it did not actually help to precipitate it. The novel was a heavy-breathing bestseller about King Louis XIV's love affair with Mademoiselle de la Vallière, who became his mistress in 1661. Ostensibly, this historical fiction had catered to the Empress Josephine, who was known to be particularly fond of romantic stories involving the royals, but it was also seen as a barely veiled revelation of the author's own notorious affair with and political aspirations for the Duke of Orleans and, after his execution, for his son,

70. *Detail of Jamet for François Kettinger Manuf.,* La Vie de Jeanne d'Arc *(The Life of Joan of Arc, 1412-1431), 1817 or later, after Charles A. Chasselat (1782-1843), Bolbec, France. Chasselet's design was copied and produced by several printed textiles firms in France, but it is unclear which factory was the first to manufacture the design. It may have been Hartmann in Munster, because Chasselat was known to have designed textiles in Munster early in his career.*

65

71. *Attributed to E. Feldtrappe (dates unknown) for unidentified manuf.,* The Seasons and Ages of Man, *1820s or 30s(?), possibly Deville (near Rouen), engraved roller print. While this textile is unsigned, there is a very close, if not identical, example at Cooper-Hewitt, printed with the signature of Feldtrappe. As with the many close variants of the Joan of Arc toile design, copies or multiple versions proliferated in later toile production, often making it difficult to determine the area of manufacture.*

Louis-Philippe, future king of France. As such, it foreshadowed the restoration of the Bourbon monarchy and the advent of a retrospective taste in the literary, visual, and performance arts that came to be known as "Troubadour." Characterized by anecdotal scenes drawn from medieval and Renaissance history, "Troubadour-style" arts indulged a fascination with intimate, historicizing details of costume, architecture, and décor.

In this vein, Madame de Genlis wrote another politically timed historical novel in 1816, this one about the medieval Maid of Orleans, Jeanne d'Arc. In retelling her triumphs for the French crown, the author contributed to the revival of her popularity as a national symbol for the Bourbon restoration. The book also helped inspire another Troubadour-style toile, designed in 1817 by Charles Chasselat (1782-1843). His pattern, produced by François Kettinger in

Bolbec, was an instant success, and it was quickly copied by other textile printers in Rouen and Alsace **(fig. 70)**.[30] If the nostalgic toiles featuring the loves of the Sun King, as well as the exploits of St. Joan, sent a clear signal that printed textile design was headed in a distinctly different direction from its Rococo and Neoclassical precedents, they also heralded the upheaval that the printed textile industry would experience following Oberkampf's death.

The key centers for production were shifting north, away from the Paris area to Rouen and Bolbec in Normandy, and also eastward to towns like Mulhouse, Munster, and Colmar in Alsace. Allied with the Swiss confederation until Alsace was reattached to France in 1798, Mulhouse had remained a free city unaffected by the prohibitions on printed cloth. It was there, as early as 1746, that the textile printer J. J. Schmaltzer teamed with the painter Jean-Henri Dollfus and the merchant Samuel Koechlin to found the region's first printed textile works. The many factories that followed ultimately turned Alsace into a world leader in the manufacture of printed cloth, and some of the original firms, Koechlin and Schlumberger, for example, are still in business today (see note 29). Nevertheless, so long as Oberkampf dominated the industry, Alsatian manufacturers generally did not try to compete in the arena of grand, pictorial furnishing toiles. Instead, they channeled their efforts to excel in the quality of their printed dyes, and they developed a specialized niche business for printing handkerchiefs. During the eighteenth century, it had been the mechanization of textile printing that most affected its growth and transformed it into a formidable economic force that led the Industrial Revolution. In the nineteenth century, it was technological development in the chemistry of fabric dyeing

that carried the industry to further heights. In the last chapter we cited Samuel Widmer's breakthrough in printing the color green. By 1815, the innovative research and development that had kept Oberkampf in the forefront was increasingly assumed by the Alsatian arm of the industry. The Alsatians first formulated the synthetic dyes that so radically transformed the character of printed cloth after the middle of the nineteenth century.

Hartmann had chosen a striking black and mustard color scheme for Lebert's *Four Elements* **(fig. 58)**. The colors stand in sharp contrast to the reds and blues of the earlier printed toiles, and attest to the particular skill that the Alsatians had with dyes. An even later textile, *The Seasons and the Ages of Man*, signed by E. Feldtrappe (dates unknown) and probably produced in Deville near Rouen **(fig. 71)**, was also printed in the fashionable ochre family of tones. But how different this design looks from Lebert's compositions! It is so claustrophobically crammed with narrative and decorative elements that the artist himself felt the need to incorporate discrete inscribed banners into the design to ensure that we do not miss the point of his theme. Sadly, the savings in time and subsequently in money provided by engraved roller printing, along with the other technological advances of the nineteenth century, were accompanied by a general decline in the quality of narrative design. Too often, the creators of these later patterns tended to transpose their models wholesale from popular engravings without attention to their harmonious integration in the overall design. The resulting adaptations on fabric, usually presented in discrete islands floating on finely patterned backgrounds, lacked the graceful, inventive blending of ideas and motifs that had so distinguished the earlier French and English copperplate-printed toiles.

67

Epilogue

Time swifly flees,
And wish'd Eternity, approaching, brings
Life undecaying, Love without Allay,
Pure flowing Joy, and Happiness sincere.

James Thomson, "Winter," The Seasons

72. Detail of J. P. Meiller Manuf., Diane et Endymion, *early 1790s (see figs. 16, 26-28).*

73. *Jean-Baptiste Huët for Oberkampf Manuf.,* Diane et Endymion, *detail of fig. 6, c. 1787, pen and ink with wash*

Amid his Subjects safe,
Slumbers the Monarch-Swain: his careless Arm
Thrown round his Head, on down Moss sustain'd
Here laid his Scrip, with wholesome Viands fill'd;
There, listening evey Noise, his watchful Dog
    James Thomson "Summer." The Seasons

69

74. *Engraving tools and copper plate from the J.P. Meillier factory at Beautiran, near Bordeaux, c. 1790. Jouy-en-Josas, France. The plate is engraved with the design known as* Diane et Endymion *(see figs. 16, 26-28, 72).*

In toiles designs undoubtedly intended for bedroom décor, the beautiful shepherd Endymion slumbers on into eternity as the seasons roll by year after year; but granted perpetual youth by Diana, he is visited in his dreams by the goddess **(figs. 72-73)**. After about 1830, the production of charming furnishing cottons printed with quaint monochromatic scenes gradually slid into obscurity, as a wide range of synthetic dyes became available and a succession of new fashion trends in interior design took their place. But they were not out of season for long. By the beginning of the twentieth century a lively interest in the tradition of *toiles-de-Jouy* was rekindled in France and America by research, publications, and exhibitions curated by the scholar and museum director Henri Clouzot, who was also a major collector of printed textiles. In the 1950s, his torch was passed to Peter Floud, keeper at the Victoria and Albert Museum in London, then to Florence Montgomery at the Henry Francis du Pont Winterthur Museum, Delaware. From the 1970s, curators in France were instrumental in establishing museums specifically dedicated to printed textiles produced in their country's great early centers of production—Jouy-en-Josas, Nantes, Rouen, and Mulhouse—and in 1989, the definitive work, *Toiles de Jouy*, was published in French and English by the curator at Jouy-en-Josas, Josette Brédif.[32] Today, fabric houses are reproducing many of the original designs, while new research continues to expand our knowledge and provide opportunities to retell some of the forgotten stories printed on cloth. Old-fashioned printed toile patterns are everywhere in the contemporary marketplace: on clothing, lingerie, handbags, sheets and bed covers, furniture upholstery, even children's dress and shower curtains.

75. *Detail from the pattern reproduced in fig. 42: Demeter, the ancient Corn goddess from Huët for Oberkampf,* Les Losanges, *c. 1800.*

These toile prints may be as familiar and well loved now as they were when they appeared in the mid-eighteenth century. Certainly, they bring us fresh insights into a bygone era, when French and English aristocrats and the sophisticated well-to-do longed for the imagined simplicity and charm of country living, and reassured themselves of their place in an ordered cyclical universe through the sprightly decoration they added to the fabric of domestic life

Appendix

The first design for a printed textile that Jean-Baptiste Huët drew for Christophe Oberkampf, *Les Travaux de la manufacture* (The Factory in Operation), is their most important collaboration for many reasons **(fig. 76)**.[33] It was commissioned to commemorate the definitive event in the manufacturer's career to that point: Louis XVI and Marie Antoinette's tour of the factory at Jouy-en-Josas in 1783. Following their visit, the King granted Oberkampf the privilege and patent protection of distinguishing all of his products with the stamp, "Manufacture Royale," which bestowed the highest approval in the realm (the letters of patent from Versailles are dated June 19, 1783). Toiles printed with this stamp were available before the end of that momentous year, marking the beginning of a lifetime collaboration between the manufacturer and the artist.

This design is also important because it provides a uniquely authentic visual record of company personnel and the procedures of woodblock and copperplate printing as they were actually practiced at Jouy-en-Josas **(figs. 3 and 74)**. As we have seen, most toile designs were based on engraved models. *Les Travaux de la manufacture* is exceptional because Huët drew it on-site, sketching his direct observations of work and life at the factory.[34] Each step in the process is accurately represented. The scenes are:[35]

Top row left to right:
1   A building in the factory complex
2   At river's edge, workers beat bundles of wet, undyed cotton that have been soaked on a floating raft
3   Woodblock printing by hand with a "color boy" assisting
4   A dye press
5   Preparing the dye
Second row:
6   The dung bath, used to remove excess mordants and unabsorbed dyes
7   Copperplate press printing a fabric marked with the arms of the King and "Manufacture Royale de S-D & Oberkampf"— an abbreviation of the names in the

manufacturer's first *chef-de-pièce*, which read in full: "MANUFACTURE DE S.D.M. OBERKAMPF MFR COMPAGNIE A JOUY EN JOSAS BON TEINT." The initials that appeared with Oberkampf's belonged to his partner, the lawyer Sarrasin de Maraise. *Les Travaux de la manufacture* was the first textile printed at Jouy-en-Josas bearing the stamp of the Royal privilege.
8   Bell for calling the employees to work
9   Village of Jouy-en-Josas with its church and textiles sun-bleaching in the fields
Third row:
10   The *lissoir*, or glazing press, used for finishing the printed cloth
11   The calendaring press (a mixture of starch and wax was applied to the printed fabric which was then passed through a series of rollers to thin and smooth it); subsequently, it was polished to a glossy finish with an agate stone.
12   The retouchers (or pencillors) supervised by the engraver, Ulrich Bossert; they are applying indigo where blues are needed and correcting any areas of imperfect printing.
Fourth row from center:
13   A designer (probably Huët) working under the eyes of the designer and plant overseer, Ludwig Rordorf
14   Oberkampf with his small son, Christophe, greeting two factory workers
15   Rinsing fabric in the Bièvre River
Fifth row:
16   The flower painter and designer, Mlle. Jouannon (Peigné), at her drawing board with Versailles seen in the distance
17   Laying out printed cotton to bleach in the sun in front of the drying house
18   The boiling dye bath with its furnaces. (The root of the madder plant produced shades of red from pink to purples, brown, and black; the weld plant produced yellow and olive colors.)

76. *Jean-Baptiste Huët for Oberkampf Manuf.,* Les Travaux de la manufacture *(The Factory in Operation), 1783-1784. Today the Braquenié division of Pierre Frey still reproduces this famous early design.*

Notes

1. James Thomson, The Seasons (Perth, Scotland: R. Morison and Son, 1793). "Winter" was published under the auspices of the bookseller John Millan when Thomson moved to London in 1726; "Summer" and "Spring" followed over the next two years, but "Autumn" did not appear in print until its inclusion in the first complete edition of *The Seasons* in 1730. The poet made revisions in 1744 and 1746, when the final version of the text was published.

2. Leonie von Wilckens, *Die textilen Künste von der Spätantike bis um 1500* (Munich, 1991), 168, fig. 188. See chap. 6, 159-172, for bibliography and a description of early European woodcuts on cloth. My appreciation goes to Elizabeth Cleland for this reference on early woodcuts, and also to Xavier Peticol for his illuminating research on figure 2: Xavier Peticol, Auction Catalogue Hôtel Drouot, Paris, 9-22-1990, p. 32, no. 113.

3. The set of nine chiaroscuro woodcuts on silk was presented by the Italian printmaker Andrea Andreani (1558/59-1629) to Vincenzo IV Gonzaga to commemorate the *Triumphs of Caesar* (1485-94), a cycle of paintings commissioned by his ancestor from Andrea Mantegna (1431-1506), preserved today at Hampton Court, England. Examples of these unusual printed silks survive at the Fogg Art Museum, Cambridge, Massachusetts; the Cleveland Museum of Art; and the Metropolitan Museum of Art, New York.

4. In France, royal prohibition of the printing and possession of printed cotton lasted from 1686 to1759. In England, the bans on cotton began in 1721 and were less strictly enforced; the Manchester Act of 1736 legalized printing on fustian (the French called it *siamoise*), a fabric woven with a linen warp and a cotton weft. In 1774, an act of Parliament legalized the use of cotton, provided that three blue threads were woven into the selvedge to indicate its English manufacture. The presence of these blue threads can prove useful in identifying English copies of French designs; conversely, their absence when selvedge has not been cut off indicates the possibility of a French copy of an English design.

5. Nadine Orenstein, "Who Took the King of Sweden to Bed?" *Print Quarterly*, 8, no. 1 (March 1991): 44-47.

6. Huët's cartoon, undoubtedly for Oberkampf, was intended for a printed textile that was never realized, most likely because the repeating design would have given the effect of unattractively heavy stripes. My thanks go to Charles Newton, Victoria and Albert Museum, who suggested the possibility of this flaw and kindly helped me construct a model to prove the theory. This design may have been Oberkampf's response to a toile produced at the Petitpierre firm in Nantes in the latter 1780s that bore a version of Aurora by the Italian painter Guido Reni (1575-1642). See Musée de l'Impression sur Étoffes, Mulhouse. *Toiles de Nantes des XVIII et XIX siècles*, exh. cat. (Mulhouse, l977-78), 42-43, no. 18.

7. For the most recent overview and bibliography on the history of cotton textiles and colorfast printing, see David Jenkins, ed., *The Cambridge History of Western Textiles*, vols. 1-2 (Cambridge, 2003). The classic references on the subject remain Serge Chassagne and Stanley D. Chapman, *European Textile Printers in the Eighteenth Century: A Study of Peel and Oberkampf* (London, 1981), and Josette Brédif, *Printed French Fabrics. Toiles des Jouy* (Paris, 1989). The most recent source, Melanie Riffel and Sophie Rouart, *Toile de Jouy. Printed Textiles in the Classic French Style* (New York, 2003), is beautifully illustrated.

8. Around 1757, at Phippsbridge in Surrey, Nixon joined George Amyand to set up a business printing fabric with engraved copperplates. Among some of the leading names to follow suit in the area around London were John Collins, John Munns, and the Quakers, Benjamin Ollive and his partner, Talwin, who founded the firm of Bromley Hall. By 1774, when the English Parliament finally lifted the country's ban on printed cotton, the hub for these manufacturers was already shifting to the area around Lancaster.

9. Sadly, no images of these rooms survive. One of Christophe Oberkampf's first jobs when he arrived in France in 1758, and worked for a Parisian cotton printer named Cottin, was the creation of an *indienne* (a woodblock-printed floral toile) for Madame de Pompadour. See *Oberkampf et la mode imprimée. Oberkampf créateur de la toile de Jouy,* cat. for the dual exhibition (Jouy-en-Josas: Musée de la Toile de Jouy and Paris: Station de métro Oberkampf, 2002).

10. Another close copy, but with a forged Jones signature, has been recently discovered; see Starr Siegele, "Old Ford Forgery," *Rotunda* 34, no. 3 (Spring 2002): 4. For information on Jones and the early English manufacturers, see Wendy Hefford, *The Victoria & Albert Museum's Textile Collection. Design for Printed Textiles in England from 1750-1850* (New York, 1992).

11. Protestant textile workers had fled France in 1685 when the revocation of the Edict of Nantes ended religious freedom and the cotton prohibition began. In their absence, the French textile industry stagnated. But after the restoration of religious freedom, Protestants returning to France were able to build a formidable new industry in printing cottons.

12. The primary source on Oberkampf and his factory is his family's archives for the business, recently put on temporary deposit at the Fondation pour l'histoire de la haute banque, Paris. It contains a copy of Gottlieb Widmer's manuscript, "Mémorial de la manufacture de Jouy," recollections of the early factory that Oberkampf's great-nephew recorded in 1854.

13. Jean-Jacques Rousseau, *Julie, or the New Heloise: The Collected Writings of Rousseau*, vol. 6, pt. 5 (Hanover, N.H., 1997), 474. Rousseau's writings incited a new market in child-rearing manuals and books for children's instruction. Among the groundbreaking contributors was Madame de Genlis, whose writings also inspired toile designs (see below) and who befriended Rousseau early in her career. A complete listing of publications and an enjoyable introduction to this prolific author, whose work ranged from educational and moral guides to history, fiction, literary criticism of women writers, biography, and autobiography, may be found in Violet Wyndham, *Madame de Genlis: A Biography* (London, 1958).

14. Jean-Michel Moreau le Jeune (1741-1814) designed both the model for the titular motif in this textile—the commemorative print picturing the tomb of the revered citizen of Geneva—and also the Marly fashion plate cited above. Given the strong connections and mutual support among the Swiss expatriates living around Paris, Oberkampf must have known the engraver Freudenberger and the Swiss Protestant banker, A. M. Eberts, a financial backer of early fashion publications. Prints by other artists in this Swiss community provided subjects for several of Oberkampf's textiles. Girardin's treatise on landscape gardening was published in Geneva in 1777 as *Composition des paysages* and in an English translation titled *An Essay on Landscape or, On the means of improving and embellishing the country round our habitation* (London, 1783).

15. For bibliography and recent research on Huët, see Laure Hug, "Jean-Baptiste Huët and the Decorative Arts," *The Magazine Antiques* 72, no. 2 (August 2002): 54-61; Laure Hug, *Catalogue raisonné de l'oeuvre peint de Jean-Baptiste Huët (1745-1811)*, DEA diss., Université de Paris IV, Sorbonne, Paris, 1997; and Laure Hug, *Recherches sur le peintre Jean-Batiste Huët (1745-1811)*, MA thesis, Université de Paris IV, Sorbonne, 1995-96. For Huët's graphic sources, see Starr Siegele, "Tales in Textiles," *Rotunda* 34, no. 2 (Winter 2001): 20-27.

16. Huët's prints after Teniers and Wouwerman were by Jacques-Philippe Le Bas (1707-1783), Justus Dankerts (1613-about 1686), and Jacques Aliamet (1726-1788). In *The Four Seasons*, his Maypole dance and grape and grain harvests are based on Pastorales engraved by Claudine Bouzonnet-Stella (1636-1697) after drawings by her uncle Jacques Stella (1596-1657).

17. For early cotton-printing centers, see Hefford, *Victoria & Albert Museum's Textile Collection*, and Henri Clouzot and Frances Morris, *Painted and Printed Fabrics. The History of the Manufactory at Jouy and Other Ateliers in France 1760-1815 [and] Notes on the History of Cotton Printing Especially in England and America* (New York, The Metropolitan Museum of Art, 1927).

18. On Nantes, see J. Jacqué, V. de Bruignac, and P. Arizzoli-Clémentel, *Toiles de Nantes des XVIII et XIX Siécles*, exh. cat. (Mulhouse: Musée de l'Impression sur Étoffes, Mulhouse, 1977-78); Bernard Roy, *Une Capitale de l'Indiennage: Nantes* (Nantes: Musée des Salorges, 1948).

19. According to the entry for this textile in the 1978 Nantes exhibition catalogue cited above (p. 40, no. 17), Pierre Dubern first printed this design about 1790, and Dubey (first name unknown) printed a second run about 1810 during their later association. Diana also appears in figures 6, 68, and 69 in another of her guises as the moon goddess, Luna.

20. E.g., William Hamilton, British ambassador to Naples in 1764-1800, published a catalogue of his own holdings: *Collection of Etruscan, Greek and Roman Antiquities from the Cabinet of the Hon.ble Wm. Hamilton, His Britannick Majesty's envoy Extraordinary at the Court of Naples*, 2 vols., 1766-67, which widely influenced the arts. For Robert Adam's relation to early Neoclassical textile design in France, see Eileen Harris, "Robert Adam and the Gobelins," *Apollo* 76, no. 2 (April 1962): 100-106.

21. A power-driven machine for engraved roller printing works with three rollers turning against one another: the engraved copper roller with the design is positioned in the middle and receives dye from a smaller feeder-roller in a tray below; a scraper automatically cleans the surface of this copper roller, leaving dye only in the engraved lines. The cloth to be printed is continuously propelled through the mechanism by a large roller positioned on top of the three, and it passes under pressure over the continuously charged copper roller beneath it. For diagrams and detailed descriptions of the various techniques involved in textile printing, see Joyce Storey, *The Thames and Hudson Manual of Textile Printing* (London, 1974).

22. My gratitude goes to Gillian Moss, retired Curator of Textiles, Cooper-Hewitt National Design Museum, Smithsonian Institution, for sharing her painstaking observations on the distinctions between copperplate and engraved roller printing.

23. *Le lion amoureux* or *Léda* (The Loving Lion or Leda and the Swan), designed by Jean-Baptiste Huët, manufactured by Oberkampf at Jouy-en-Josas, 1808. Surviving examples printed in green are in Paris at the Bibliothèque Forney (acc. no. 181172) and in Toronto at the Royal Ontario Museum (acc. no. 934.4.528).

24. Most significant was Raphael, *Loggie di Raphael nel Vaticano*, Rome, 1772 [1770?]-1777 (engraved by Giovanni Volpato and Giovanni Ottaviani after the drawings of Pietro Camporesi and Ludovico Tesco under the general editorship of Gaetano

75

Savorelli). Oberkampf produced a close companion for the textile reproduced in fig. 39; it is modeled on motifs in the Loggie and is reproduced in Riffel and Rouart, *Toile de Jouy*, 124.

25. Margaret A. Fikioris, "Neoclassicism in Textile Designs by Jean Huet," *Winterthur Portfolio* 6 (Charlottesville, Va., 1970), 84. Figure 42, *Oiseaux et écureuils*, borrows from Volpato and Ottaviani's engravings in vol. I, plates III through VI).

26. Technological advances that gave rise to the printed textile industry were part of the innovation taking place in the larger arena of printmaking in the eighteenth century, when ingenious intaglio techniques were devised to replicate chalk, pastel, watercolor and gouache drawings with ornate, decorative borders printed in real gold. The Paris firm founded by Arthur had a series of partners: to 1789 it was called Arthur & Grenard; to 1794 Arthur & Robert; to 1807 Robert et Cie. For information on the artists and work associated with the specialty aquatint print shops active in Paris during the 1790s, see Bernard Jacqué and Geert Wisse, "*Note sur un ensemble de papiers peints imprimés en taille-douce à Paris à la fin du XVIIIe siècle*," *Nouvelles de l'estampe*, sommaire nos. 124-125 (October 1992), 5-29; and notes by Alberto Milano and Peter Fuhring in *Print Quarterly* 6, no. 3 (September 1989): 313-314; 7, no. 1 (March 1990): 56-57; 8, no. 3 (September 1991): 284-295. In the personal journal of the Colmar textile designer, Henri Lebert (see below), there is a revealing page in which the same small intaglio plate has been printed on paper, cotton cloth, and silk, and carefully cut out and mounted. Bibliothèque Municipal, Colmar, ms B.N. *achat* 85-09 (Vol. 1, 1794-1813), 667. Relating to the medallion print in figure 43, the Royal Ontario Museum owns an example of Huët's *Les Travaux de la manufacture* (see Appendix) finished with an appliqué of the same border. My thanks goes to Jacqueline Jacqué, Director of the Musée de l'Impression sur Étoffes, Mulhouse, for identifying the intended use of Moitte's satin prints as chairbacks.

27. My dating and attribution of the Cooper-Hewitt drawings to Marie-Bonaventure Lebert, rather than to his younger brother, Jean-Baptiste (1760-1873), also an engraver and designer, is secured by annotations on a variant set of drawings I discovered in a journal kept by the Marie-Bonaventure Lebert's son, Henri: Bibliothèque Municipal, Colmar, ms B.N. *achat* 85-09 (vol. 1, 1794-1813), 131, 133, 135, 137.

28. The textile in figure 54 can be broadly dated to 1799-1818 because its factory mark was in use then. The mark appears on an example of the textile at the Musée de l'Impression sur Étoffes in Mulhouse (acc. no. 858.127.1).

29. In 1991, Pierre Frey acquired the concern, agreeing to keep the Braquenié label associated with the grand old designs, many of which are still reproduced today. For houses printing contemporary versions of the early patterns, see the appendices in Riffel and Rouart, and Judith Straeten, *Toiles de Jouy* (Salt Lake City, Utah, 2002).

30. There is a cartoon signed and dated "Chasselat, Paris, 1817" at the Cooper-Hewitt National Design Museum, Smithsonian Institution, 1898-21-27. Madame de Genlis, *Jeanne de France. Nouvelle historique*, 2 vols. (Paris, 1816).

31. The enchanting design in figure 68 has long been credited to the Petitpierre brothers' firm in Nantes. However, no examples are known with a Nantes factory mark, and we believe now that it more likely originated in Beautiran, in Bordeaux, a town of less distinguished printed textile production than the bigger centers. Publication is forthcoming of several curators' collaborative research with Xavier Peticol, who has addressed narrative subjects in textiles printed around Beautiran in two exhibitions for that community: Xavier Peticol, *Visages du Pays de l'Aruan*, exh. cat. (Beautiran, 1982), and Guy Crevelli and Xavier Peticol, *Indiennes et toiles imprimées de Beartiran et de France aux XVIIIe et XIXe siècles* (Beautiran, 1989). Why the Diana and Endymion story, which was a popular subject among artists, seems to appear nowhere else in printed textiles adds to the interest of this design, which I will address in an upcoming article.

32. Musée de la toile de Jouy, Jouy-en-Josas; Musée de l'Impression sur Étoffes, Mulhouse; Musée de Château des Ducs de Bretagne, Nantes.

33. *Les Travaux de la Manufacture* continued its popularity over the years. The Allentown Art Museum owns a close reproduction, which was reproduced in the 1930s with a factory mark in the selvedge that reads: "Manuf. Royal de LM & Oberkampf." Since 1994 (and their merger with Braquenié) the firm of Pierre Frey has been reproducing this famous design from Braquenié's archive of early Oberkampf factory documents, with their contemporary version engraved by Gandit and printed by Mermoz. See Monelle Hayot, "*La maison d'Oberkampf réinventée en Braquenié*," *Demeure historique* 132, no. 1, (1ère trimestre, 1999): 30-31, and Jacques Sirat, Anne de Thoisy, and Serge Chassagne, *Quand Braquenié rencontre Oberkampf: L'Objet d'art* hors-série no. 332 (January 1999), 38 and endpages.

34. I recently identified two of the artist's preparatory studies for the design: one, of the furnace tender next to a steeping vat, is in St. Petersburg at The Hermitage, OP23839; the other is a study for the plant manager who stands in the textile design overseeing a seated draftsman—most likely Huët himself (sold at Sotheby's, New York, 1/27/99, lot 225).

35. My appreciation goes to Christa Thurman, The Christa C. Mayer Thurman Curator of Textiles, Art Institute of Chicago, for identifying and mapping the activities at the factory as seen here.

Credits

Endpapers Chicago, IL., The Art Institute of Chicago, Gift of Mrs. Potter Palmer, II, 1949.955.

Title page Allentown, Pa., Allentown Art Museum, Purchase: The Reverend and Mrs. Van S. Merle-Smith, Jr. Endowment Fund, 2002. (2002.5.35). Photograph by Robert Walch.

Frontispiece Allentown Art Museum, Purchase: The Kate Fowler Merle-Smith Memorial Fund, 1988. (1988.7). Photograph by Robert Walch.

Endpiece Allentown Art Museum, Purchase: The Reverend and Mrs. Van S. Merle-Smith, Jr. Endowment Fund, 2002. (2002.5.35.). Photograph by Robert Walch.

1. Musée de la Toile de Jouy, 994.1.1. Photograph by Christophe Walter.
2. Allentown Art Museum, Purchase: The Reverend and Mrs. Van S. Merle-Smith, Jr. Endowment Fund, 2002. (2002.05.15). Photograph by Robert Walch.
3. New York, N.Y.,Cooper-Hewitt National Design Museum, Smithsonian Institution: Purchased for the Museum by the Advisory Council, 1925-1-367.
4. Washington, D.C., National Gallery of Art: . Rosenwald Collection, 1949.5.81. Image © Board of Trustees, National Gallery of Art.
5. Allentown Art Museum, Purchase: The Reverend and Mrs. Van S. Merle-Smith, Jr. Endowment Fund, 1996. (1996.3). Photograph by Robert Walch.
6. Allentown Art Museum, Purchase: Gift of Claire L. Siegele and Starr Siegele in Memory of Louise Starr, 1990. (1990.17). Photograph by Robert Walch.
7. Chicago, Il., The Newberry Library.
8. Allentown Art Museum, Purchase: The Kate Fowler Merle-Smith Memorial Fund, 1988. (1988.7). Photograph by Robert Walch.
9. Cooper-Hewitt, National Design Museum, Smithsonian Institution: Museum purchase from General Acquisitions Fund, 1984.97.1. Photograph by Matt Flynn.
10. Toronto, Canada, with permission of the Royal Ontario Museum, © ROM 967.176.1.
11. Cooper-Hewitt, National Design Museum, Smithsonian Institution: Gift of Mrs. Robert P. Brown, 1960-81-9.
12. New York, N.Y., The Metropolitan Museum of Art: Rogers Fund, 1983, 1983.365. Photograph © 1983 The Metropolitan Museum of Art.
13. Musée de la Toile de Jouy: 992.5.7.a-l. Photograph by Gérard Dufrene.
14. Musée de la Toile de Jouy, gift of the Baronne Mallet, 976.1.1.a-c. Photograph by Christoph Walter.
15. Photograph courtesy of Starr Siegele.
16. Allentown Art Museum, Purchase: The Reverend and Mrs. Van S. Merle-Smith, Jr. Endowment Fund, 2002. (2002.05.1). Photograph by Robert Walch.
17. Allentown Art Museum, Purchase: The Reverend and Mrs. Van S. Merle-Smith, Jr. Endowment Fund, 2002. (2002.5.50).Photograph by Robert Walch.
18. With permission of the Royal Ontario Museum © ROM 934.4.441.
19-20 The Metropolitan Museum of Art, Gift of William Sloane Coffin, 1926, 26.265.25 Photograph © 2001 The Metropolitan Museum of Art.
21. Photograph courtesy of Starr Siegele.
22. Musée de la Toile de Jouy: 997.5.2.b. Photograph by Marc Walter.
23. The Newberry Library, Chicago.
24. Allentown Art Museum, Purchase: The Kate Fowler Merle-Smith Memorial Fund, 1988. (1988.7).Photograph by Robert Walch.
25. The Art Institute of Chicago, Gift of Mrs. Howell B. Erminger, 1965.776a-b. Reproductions nos. 25, 43, 44, 60, 69, 71 courtesy of The Art Institute of Chicago.
26. Allentown Art Museum, Purchase: The Reverend and Mrs. Van S. Merle-Smith, Jr. Endowment Fund, 2002. (2002.5.1). Photograph by Robert Walch.
27. Allentown Art Museum, Purchase: The Reverend and Mrs. Van S. Merle-Smith, Jr. Endowment Fund, 2002. (2002.5.1). Photograph by Robert Walch.
28. Allentown Art Museum, Purchase: The Reverend and Mrs. Van S. Merle-Smith, Jr. Endowment Fund, 2002. (2002.5.1). Photograph by Robert Walch.
29. Allentown Art Museum, Purchase: Gift in Memory of Kate Fowler Merle-Smith, 1983. (1983.05.2.1). Photograph by Robert Walch.
30. Allentown Art Museum, Purchase: The Reverend and Mrs. Van S. Merle-Smith, Jr. Endowment Fund, 2002. (2002.5.16). Photograph by Robert Walch.
31. Allentown Art Museum, Purchase: The Reverend and Mrs. Van S. Merle-Smith, Jr. Endowment Fund, 2002. (2002.5.45). Photograph by Robert Walch.
32. Allentown Art Museum, Purchase: The Reverend and Mrs. Van S. Merle-Smith, Jr. Endowment Fund, 2002. (2002.5.60). Photograph by Robert Walch.

33. Allentown Art Museum, Purchase: Gift in Memory of Kate Fowler Merle-Smith, 1983. (1983.05.3). Photograph by Robert Walch.
34. The Newberry Library, Chicago.
35. Allentown Art Museum, Purchase: The Kate Fowler Merle-Smith Memorial Fund, 1988. (1988.7). Photograph by Robert Walch.
36. Wadsworth Atheneum, Harford, CT: Gift of Mrs. Edward S. Boyd, 1928.23.
37. Cooper-Hewitt, National Design Museum, Smithsonian Institution: Museum purchase from the Au Panier Fleuri Fund, 1957-51-1-a. Photograph by Ken Pelka.
38. Allentown Art Museum, Purchase: The Reverend and Mrs. Van S. Merle-Smith, Jr. Endowment Fund, 2002. (2002.5.53). Photograph by Robert Walch.
39. Allentown Art Museum, Purchase: The Reverend and Mrs. Van S. Merle-Smith, Jr. Endowment Fund, 2002. (2002.5.43). Photograph by Robert Walch.
40. Allentown Art Museum, Purchase: The Reverend and Mrs. Van S. Merle-Smith, Jr. Endowment Fund, 2002. (2002.5.5). Photograph by Robert Walch.
41. Cooper-Hewitt, National Design Museum, Smithsonian Institution: Gift of Cora Ginsburg, 1994-80-15.
42. Allentown Art Museum, The Reverend and Mrs. Van S. Merle-Smith, Jr. Endowment Fund, 2002. (2002.5.7). Photograph by Robert Walch.
43. The Art Institute of Chicago: Edward M. Cummings Endowment, 1990.526
44. The Art Institute of Chicago: Ryerson and Burnham Libraries, 724.15 V34rl.: Photograph by Greg Williams.
45. Allentown Art Museum, Purchase: The Reverend and Mrs. Van S. Merle-Smith, Jr. Endowment Fund, 2002. (2002.5.63). Photograph by Robert Walch.
46. Allentown Art Museum, Purchase: The Reverend and Mrs. Van S. Merle-Smith, Jr. Endowment Fund, 2002. (2002.5.3). Photograph by Robert Walch.
47. Allentown Art Museum, Purchase: The Reverend and Mrs. Van S. Merle-Smith, Jr. Endowment Fund, 2002. (2002.05.63). Photograph by Robert Walch.
48. Allentown Art Museum: on Loan From a Private Collection.
49. Cooper-Hewitt, National Design Museum, Smithsonian Institution: Bequest of Richard Cranch Greenleaf in memory of this mother, Adeline Emma Greenleaf, 1962-54-16. Photograph by Steve Tague.
50. Cooper-Hewitt, National Design Museum, Smithsonian Institution: Bequest of Richard Cranch Greenleaf in memory of this mother, Adeline Emma Greenleaf, 1962-54-17. Photograph by Steve Tague.
51. Allentown Art Museum, Purchase: SOTA Print Fund, 2000. (2000.4). Photograph by Robert Walch.
52. Allentown Art Museum, Purchase: SOTA Print Fund, 1999. (1999.21.2). Photograph by Robert Walch.
53. Allentown Art Museum, Purchase: SOTA Print Fund, 2003. (2003.5.1). Photograph by Robert Walch.
54. Allentown Art Museum, Purchase: SOTA Print Fund, 2003. (2003.5.2). Photograph by Robert Walch.
55. Cooper-Hewitt, National Design Museum, Smithsonian Institution: Gift of Bridget Mahon, 1898.21.6b.
56. Baltimore, MD., The Baltimore Museum of Art: Gift of Dena S. Katzenberg, BMA 1984.180.
57. Cooper-Hewitt, National Design Museum, Smithsonian Institution: Gift of Bridget Mahon, 1898.21.6a.
58. Allentown Art Museum, Purchase: Gift of Kate Fowler Merle-Smith, by Exchange, 1979. (1979.3.1) Photograph by Robert Walch.
59. Allentown Art Museum, Purchase: The Reverend and Mrs. Van S. Merle-Smith, Jr. Endowment Fund, 2002 (2002.5.12). Photograph by Robert Walch.
60. The Art Institute of Chicago: Restricted gift of Mrs. Martha Borland Willis in memory of Mrs. Chauncey B. Borland, 1981.54.
61-66. Cooper-Hewitt, National Design Museum, Smithsonian Institution: Gift of Bridget Mahon: 61. 1898-21-12a: 62. 1898-21-13; 63. 1898-21-11; 64. 1898-21-12b; 65. 1898-21-10a and 10c; 66. 1898-21-10b. Photographs by Matt Flynn.
67. The Newberry Library, Chicago.
68. Allentown Art Museum, Purchase: The Kate Fowler Merle-Smith Memorial Fund, 1988. (1988.7). Photograph by Robert Walch.
69. The Art Institute of Chicago: Gift of Emily Crane Chadbourne, 1952.650.
70. Allentown Art Museum: Gift of Jeanette Werner, 1979 (1979.2.1.1). Photograph by Robert Walch.
71. The Art Institute of Chicago: Gift of Emily Crane Chadbourne, 1952.648.
72. Allentown Art Museum, Purchase: The Reverend and Mrs. Van S. Merle-Smith, Jr. Endowment Fund, 2002. (2002.5.2). Photograph by Robert Walch.
73. New York, Cooper-Hewitt National Design Museum, Smithsonian Institution. Museum purchase from General Acquisitions Fund, 1984-97-1.
74. Musée de la Toile de Jouy, on loan from the Musée Lambinet, Versailles. Photograph by Marc Walter pour le Musée de la Toile de Jouy.
75. Allentown Art Museum, Purchase: The Reverend and Mrs. Van S. Merle-Smith, Jr. Endowment Fund, 2002. (2002.5.6). Photograph by Robert Walch.
76. Musée de la Toile de Jouy: Gift of Mlle.Biver, 978.1.6a. Photograph by Marc Walter

Acknowledgments

Many treasured colleagues and friends have aided and encouraged my study of early printed textiles:

The fundamental idea to consider pictures specifically designed for printed fabric patterns from the viewpoint of a print specialist belongs to Christa C. Thurman. As longtime curator, conservator, and head of the Department of Textiles at the Art Institute of Chicago, Mrs. Thurman oversees one of the prime collections of early printed cottons. Her inspiration and dedication to realizing this project was instrumental in the emergence of a new hybrid field of study and the estabishment of the first comprehensive database for the models used by toile designers.

During the writing of this book, the Antonio Ratti Textile Center at The Metropolitan Museum of Art provided a haven for technical and research resources; to Giovanna Fiorino-Iannace, Lisa Candage, and all the staff of the Center goes my gratitude for their constant, enthusiastic support. A remarkable treasure trove only a few blocks to the north of The Met, Cooper-Hewitt National Design Museum, Smithsonian Institution, acted as my annex. It houses the most important assemblage of works on paper related to printed cotton outside of France, and in 1995, Elinor Merrell's superb bequest of printed textiles was incorporated into their already-extensive collection. I am indebted to Gillian Moss, retired head of their Department of Textiles, for readily sharing her interest and experience in the subject, and to the present Department: Matilda McQuaid, Barbara Duggan, Susan Brown. My appreciation also goes to Lorna Filippini at the Art Institute of Chicago for continuing to lend her eyes and her expertise in textile conservation.

Colleagues in the departments of drawings and prints at many museums and libraries have been tireless in offering assistance and sharing invaluable knowledge of their collections. My gratitude goes especially to Gail Davidson, Floramae McCarron-Cates, and Marilyn Symmes (former department head) at Cooper-Hewitt and also to all of my associates at the Met (they are legion); in Chicago at the Art Institute and Newberry Library; London at the Victoria and Albert Museum and the British Museum; Paris at the École Nationale Supérieur des Beaux Arts and the Cabinet des Estampes at the Bibliothèque Nationale—by far the most valuable resource for identifying designers' models in French prints.

In France, the world-specialists in printed textiles have warmly welcomed American scholarship and generously shared their passion for *toiles-de-Jouy*. I am indebted to Madame Josette Brédif, grande doyenne of *toiles peintes*, and to Xavier Peticol, Laure Hug, Jacqueline and Bernard Jacqué, Melanie Riffel and Sophie Rouart. In London, special thanks go to Clare Browne at the V&A; in Toronto, Alexandra Palmer and her staff at the Royal Ontario Museum, and Prof. Patricia Bruckmann, the crusader who introduced my new area of research into the larger arena of eighteenth-century literary scholarship; in New York, Judith Straeten, archivist-curator at Brunschwig et Fils, and Fariba Thomson and Susan Schulman, whose kindness made possible Allentown's Merrell acquisition.

As Mr. Brigham acknowledged in the Foreword, several institutions have generously provided research grants and fellowships: the Art Institute of Chicago, Cooper-Hewitt National Design Museum, Smithsonian Institution, Royal Ontario Museum, Metropolitan Museum of Art, Oberkampf Archives at La Fondation Pour l'Histoire de la Haute Banque, and the Samuel H. Kress Foundation, where Lisa Ackermann's sustaining interest in the subject has nurtured its research in several museums and seeded the funding for this publication.

Finally and most importantly, this book owes its existence to the collaboration of Allentown Art Museum and Bunker Hill Publishing. My gratitude goes to Executive Director David Brigham and his staff: Ruta Saliklis, Christine I. Oaklander, Sophia Bakis, Shana Leigh Herb, and Carl Schafer; at Bunker Hill to Ib Bellew, Carole Kitchel, and the able design and editorial skills of Louise Millar and Karen Palmer, respectively. To Anne Hoy, whose sensitive editorial gifts helped realize my vision so beautifully, I owe special thanks. And to my main editor, collaborator, and inspiration in this project and in life, my enduring respect and appreciation goes to Larry Feinberg.

The Seasons thus,
As ceaseless round a jarring World they roll,
Still find them happy...
Till Evening comes at last, serene and mild;
..after the long vernal Day of Life...

James Thomson, "Spring," The Seasons

Detail of La Chasse de Diane *(Diana the Huntress), fig. 40. Diana sleeping with her nymphs.*